COPYRIGHT

This book was written for the benefit of all, but in order not to underestimate the rights of the authors, we must mention the source information in copying and pasting.

ABOUT OF AUTHORS

Mohammed Ridha FAISAL,

He is currently a PhD student in the Department of Computer Engineering at Suleyman Demiral University in Turkey. He was born in Baghdad in 1991,

I will happy to receive your suggestions at drengmrf@gmail.com, I are also happy to follow you and support me on social media:

⬛ : facebook.com/EngValley

:youtube.com/channel/UC___GrimRjihbtKfE-sDKg

About of the Second Author

Abdullah Ridha Faisal,

Assistant lecturer Abdullah Ridha Faisal, instructor, at Al-Nisour University college / Computer Technical Engineering , Department - Iraq - Baghdad.

I will happy to receive your suggestions at abdullah.r.eng@nuc.edu, also happy to follow you and support me on social media

https://www.youtube.com/channel/UC2aekGrimRjihbtKfE-sDKg

https://play.google.com/store/apps/details?id=com.dreng mr.abdullahridha

About of the Third Author

Nanh Ridha Faisal,

She is a PhD student in Civil Engineering in Turkey. She loves cooking and has a book on the art of cooking, as well as interested in learning all that is new in the world of technology.

About of Graphic Designer

Abdulrahman Ridha Faisal,

Was born in 2002 in Baghdad, Iraq. And he now in high School in Isparta, Turkey.

 : instgram.com/_a.ridha_

▶   :

youtube.com/channel/UC_PAmfXG41jtYyWTlzkRFtw

Muiz Ridha Faisal,

Was born in 1999 in Baghdad, Iraq. And he now in university student.

THANK YOU

I would like to thank my beloved family, especially my father and my mother, for their persistence, contribution and support in the preparation of the first edition of this book. Thanks to Muiz Faisal and Abdulraham Faisal, who also helped in photography design.

I explained the optional or secondary topics for the Department of Computer Engineering, but they are also necessary in the near future, and also important for students of higher studies, to obtain preliminary information on OPTIMIZATION, WEB PROGRAMMING, MOBILE PROGRAMMING, BASICS OF COMPUTER VISION, DEEP LEARNING, BIG DATA, DATA MINING, AND ARTIFICIAL INTELLIGENCE.

In the stage of the proficiency examination in the doctorate, he had to review the lessons and topics that I took at the university level, and it was difficult to compile all the lectures, search for a source that includes all the university lectures explaining in a simple way and without going into the topics to gain time. Unfortunately, I did not find such a book, so I decided to write two books that include university lectures for the Department of Computer Engineering, the first book includes lectures on compulsory lessons, and the second book includes lectures for elective lessons.

I have gathered book information by reading academic books that explain in depth the information, in addition to the university lecture notes I have collected. So I recommend reading the two books.

The book deals the main and compulsory lessons of the Department of Computer Engineering, in an easy, simple and adequate way to understand the topics of computer engineering and similar departments, this book is considered as a booklet for undergraduate students, and even for doctoral students, where it shortens the way for doctoral students to review the basic lessons of the Department of Computer Engineering, and Also, the way is shortened for engineering students and those interested in the Computer Department to learn the main curriculum for the department in a brief way. The book deals with topics COMPUTER NETWORKS, PROGRAMMING LANGUAGES, SOFTWARE ENGINEERING, SOFTWARE MODELING LANGUAGES AND UML, OBJECT ORIENTED PROGRAMMING, DATA STRUCTURES AND DATA MODELS, DATABASE MANAGEMENT AND SQL, DISCRETE MATHEMATICS, BOOLEAN ALGEBRA, LOGIC CIRCUITS, ALGORITHM AND FLOW CHARTS, MICROPROCESSOR, PROGRAMMING IN ASSEMBLY LANGUAGE, and OPERATING SYSTEMS.

In the second book, I explained the optional or secondary topics for the Department of Computer Engineering, but they are also necessary in the near future, and also important for students of higher studies, to obtain preliminary information on OPTIMIZATION, BASICS OF COMPUTER VISION, WEB PROGRAMMING, MOBILE PROGRAMMING, ARTIFICIAL INTELLIGENCE, DEEP LEARNING, BIG DATA, and DATA MINING. So I recommend reading the two books.

CONTENTS

6

This book is complementary to the first book "Computer Engineering on Overview : Compulsory", as we said before. In this book we will discuss additional topics for the Department of Computer Engineering and similar departments, these new topics are important at the present time and increase their importance with the passage of time and they are in a rapid development. Among these topics:

Optimization: is part of the science of algorithms, in mathematics choosing the optimal component from a set of possible candidate options. The question is formulated on the basis of maximizing the objective function or reducing the cost function. It is used in several contexts, including:

In mathematics, optimization is the branch concerned with finding the maximum and minimum ends of a mathematical function, sometimes with constraints. One example of the optimization topic is finding the maximum industrial production without exceeding the permissible limits of resources. Optimization has many applications in logistics and design problems.

In informatics, optimization is the process of improving a system's performance so that it reduces effective operating time., Bandwidth or memory requirements. Although the name is optimization (finding the optimum), it does not always mean finding the optimal solution to an issue or problem. Often this is not possible and the heuristic algorithm should be used instead of optimization.

Search Engine Optimization (SEO) is a set of methodology that aims to improve the ranking of results for sites that result from a specific search on the web.

Computer vision: is one of the fields of computer science, which aims to build smart applications capable of understanding the content of images as human beings understand them. Where image data can take many forms, such as successive images (video), scenes from several cameras, data of several dimensions taken from a medical imaging device. Digital signal processing, neuroscience and artificial intelligence. Topics include color, light and image formation; early, mid- and high-level vision; and mathematics essential for computer vision.

Web programming: Web programming refers to the writing, markup and coding involved in Web development, which includes Web content, Web client and server scripting and network security. The most common languages used for Web programming are XML, HTML, JavaScript, Perl 5 and

2

PHP. Web programming is different from just programming, which requires interdisciplinary knowledge on the application area, client and server scripting, and database technology. But the **Web development;** refer to the work involved in developing a website for the Internet (World Wide Web) or an intranet (a private network).Web development can range from developing a simple single static page of plain text to complex web-based internet applications (web apps), electronic businesses, and social network services. A more comprehensive list of tasks to which web development commonly refers, may include web engineering, web design, web content development, client liaison, client-side/server-side scripting, web server and network security configuration, and e-commerce development.

web development roadmap		
Front-End-Stack	Back-End-Stack	Full-Stack
HTML	SQL	
CSS	PHP	Front-end-stack
JavaScript	ASP	and Back-end-
	Python	stack
	Ruby	

Mobile app programming: Mobile programming refers to the writing, markup and coding involved in Mobile development, which includes Mobile UI considers constraints, contexts, screen, input, and mobility as outlines for design. The most common languages used for Mobile programming are Java, Kotlin, and C#. But the **Mobile app development;** refer to the act or process by which a mobile app is developed for mobile devices, such as personal digital assistants, enterprise digital assistants or mobile phones. These applications can be pre-installed on phones during manufacturing platforms, or delivered as web applications using server-side or client-side processing (e.g., JavaScript) to provide an "application-like" experience within a Web browser. Application software developers also must consider a long array of screen sizes, hardware specifications, and configurations because of intense competition in mobile software and changes within each of the platforms.

Artificial intelligence: is the behavior and specific characteristics of computer programs that make them mimic human mental capabilities and working patterns. Among the most important of these characteristics is the ability to learn, infer, and react to situations not programmed in the

4

machine. However, this term is controversial due to the lack of a specific definition of intelligence.

And artificial intelligence is a branch of computer science. Artificial intelligence is defined by many works as "the study and design of smart clients", and a smart customer is a system that absorbs its environment and takes situations that increase its chance of success in achieving its mission or the mission of its team.

Deep Learning: is a new field of research dealing with finding theories and algorithms that allow the machine to learn on its own by simulating neurons in the human body. And one of the branches of science that deals with artificial intelligence. Is one of the branches of machine learning science, most of the in-depth learning research focuses on finding methods of deriving a high degree of abstraction by analyzing a huge data set using linear and non-linear variables.

Discoveries in this area have proven significant, rapid and effective progress in many areas including facial recognition, speech recognition, computer vision, and natural language processing.

The machine learns from big data using different designs for deep learning networks, including: frequent networks (RNN) frequently used with continuous texts and data, and a circumferential neural network (CNN) that draws inspiration from biological processes in the visual lobe and other designs.

Big data: is a term that refers to a set of data that is difficult or bulky to store or process with a standard data management tool or application. Or simply to approximate understandings, it cannot be dealt with on a single computer alone through a simple database. One of the features of the "big data" field is the use of several computers to share the required works.

Data mining: is a computerized and manual search for knowledge of data without prior assumptions about what that knowledge might be. Data mining is also defined as the process of analyzing a quantity of data (usually a large amount), to find a logical relationship that summarizes the data in a new way that is understandable and useful to the owner of the data. Models are called relationships and summarized data obtained from data mining. Data mining usually deals with data that has been obtained for a purpose other than the purpose of data mining (for example, a

6

database of transactions in a bank), which means that the method of data mining does not affect the way the data itself is collected. This is one of the areas in which data mining differs from statistics, and for this the data mining process is referred to as a secondary statistical process. The definition also indicates that the amount of data is usually large, but in the event that the amount of data is small, it is preferable to use regular statistical methods in analyzing it.

2 OPTIMIZATION

Optimization, in its most general sense, is the process of determining the values that decision variables will take in order to optimize the value of a specified purpose function in a system, under certain constraints. In other words, it is the process of determining what system inputs and or their values will be in order to obtain a desired output.

The aim of optimizing the function can be minimization or maximization according to the type of the problem.

For example, solving a scheduling problem to minimize the number of delayed jobs is an optimization problem. Likewise, it is an optimization process to solve an assembly line balancing problem in order to minimize the number of stations or maximize line efficiency, or in order to minimize the total cost of an economic stock quantity determination problem.

The difference between simulation and optimization is,

Simulation is the process of estimating, determining the output in a system where inputs are known. For example, the simulation of a production process where the arrival time of the

orders and the

Known --------> | Known | --------> ?
         Input   Model   Output

time spent in the system is known, when the production will be completed, free time in the system, the effectiveness of the system, etc. can be estimated to a large extent.

Optimization is the process of determining the inputs or the values of these inputs in order to obtain the desired output. For example, determining what parameters of a 3D printer will be in order to achieve the desired surface roughness is an example of optimization.

? -------> | Known | --------> Known

Input   Model   Output

Techniques used in the optimization process:

Analytical Methods:

They give the optimum solution within tolerances. In large-scale problems, it takes too long to reach the result, or it cannot be achieved. Ex, mathematical modeling, branch-bound algorithm, etc.

Intuitive Methods:

They are problem-specific solution methods and follow a specific algorithm. Although they do not guarantee the optimum solution, they produce faster solutions than analytical methods. Ex, Johnson algorithm for flow type scheduling problems, position weight method for assembly line balancing problems, etc.

Meta Heuristic Methods:

They are solution methods obtained by adapting certain algorithms to the problem structure to be solved. Ex, genetic algorithm, ant colony algorithm, annealing simulation algorithm, etc.

Optimization problems:

$$\min_{x \in \mathbb{R}^n} f(x) \ \text{s.t.} \ \begin{cases} c_i(x) = 0, & i \in \mathcal{E} \\ c_i(x) \geq 0, & i \in \mathcal{I} \end{cases}$$

Equality restrictions (numerical)
Inequality constraints (numerical)

x: variables (vector); And f(x): objective (numerical) function.

Applicable area: a group of points that meet all restrictions.

$\max f \equiv -\min -f.$

- Ex. (fig. 1.1): $\min (x_1 - 2)^2 + (x_2 - 1)^2$ s.t. $\begin{cases} x_1^2 - x_2 \leq 0 \\ x_1 + x_2 \leq 2. \end{cases}$
- Ex.: transportation problem (LP)

$$\min \sum_{i,j} c_{ij} x_{ij} \ \text{s.t.} \ \begin{cases} \sum_j x_{ij} \leq a_i & \forall i \quad \text{(capacity of factory } i) \\ \sum_i x_{ij} \geq b_j & \forall i \quad \text{(demand of shop } j) \\ x_{ij} \geq 0 & \forall i,j \quad \text{(nonnegative production)} \end{cases}$$

c_{ij}: shipping cost; x_{ij}: quantity of product shipped from factory i to store j.

• Example: LSQ problem: Parametric model fit (eg line, polynomial, neural network ...) to a data set.

• Repetitive optimization algorithms: Build a sequence of points that converge with the solution. Needs a good starting point (often with prior knowledge).

• Focus on many changing problems (but will be illustrated in 2D).

• Desiderata for algorithms:

- Durability: good performance in a variety of problems in its class, for any starting point;
- Efficiency: little computer or storage time;
- Accuracy: precisely defining the solution (within the limits of fixed point calculation).

They conflict with each other.

• General Comment on Improvement (Fletcher): "An impressive blend of theory and arithmetic, reasoning and rigor."

- No global algorithm: a specific algorithm works well for a specific class of problem.

- It is necessary to adapt a method to the problem posed (by experimentation).

- Do not choose the appropriate algorithm solution ← that was found too slowly or not at all.

• Not covered in Nocedal & Wright, or in this course:

- Separate optimization (correct programming): separate variables. Example: Correct transportation issue, Street vendor problem.

  * More difficult to solve than continuous selection (in the end we can expect the value of the objective function in the nearby points).

  * Many solutions to count them.

  * gives rounding usually provides very bad solutions.

  * techniques Highly specialized techniques for each type of problem.

- Network selection: shortest paths, maximum flow, minimum cost flow, duties and matches, MST, dynamic programming, division of the graph. . .

- Non-smooth selection: disconnected derivatives, eg L1 standard.

- Stochastic random selection: the model is identified with uncertainty, for example $x \leq b$ where b can be given by probability density function.

- Global selection: Look for the global minimum, not just the local minimum. very Difficult. Some inference: simulated annealing, genetic algorithms, evolutionary computation.

- Multi-goal selection: One method is to convert it into a single goal = linear combinations of targets.

- EM (Prediction - Maximization) algorithm: a specialized technique for estimating the probability of the maximum probability models.

- Calculating differences: fixed point of a function (= function of a functions).

- Convex Optimization: We'll see some of this.

- Modeling: preparing the selection problem, that is, the process of determining the goal, the variables, and the constraints for a specific problem. Very important but depends on the application.

• Course contents: Derivative methods for continuous improvement.

Local Minimum Conditions x^* (see case n = 1) $\left[E2 \right.$

Global thumbnail: $f(x^*) \le f(x) \ \forall \ x \in R^n$.

• Local thumbnail: $\exists$ neighborhood N of x^*: $f(x^*) \le f(x) \ \forall \ x \in$ N.

• Strict (or strong) global thumbnail: $f(x^*) < f(x) \ \forall x \in N \setminus \{x^*\}$. (Example $f(x) = 3$ versus $f(x) = (x - 2)^4$ at $x^* = 2$.)

Isolated local reduction device: $\exists N$ for x^* where x^* is the local minimum only. In N. (Example $f(x) = x^4 \cos 1/x + 2x^4$ with $f(0) = 0$ it has a strict global microcosm at $x^* = 0$ but is not isolated.) Every local minute is isolated. Strict.

First Class Necessary Conditions: x^* local min, f cont. Difference. In an open neighborhood of $x^* \Rightarrow \nabla f(x^*) = 0$. (Insufficient state, for example: $f(x) = x^3$.)

(Pf: paradoxically: if $\nabla f(x^*) 6 = 0$, f decreases along the gradient direction.)

• fixed point: $\nabla f(x^*) = 0$.

• Second degree necessary conditions: x^* local minutes, f twice. Difference. In an open neighborhood of $x^* \Rightarrow \nabla f(x^*) = 0$, $\nabla 2f(x^*)$ is psd. (Insufficient state, for example: $f(x) = x^3$.)

(Pf.: Paradoxically: if $\nabla^2 f(x^*)$ is not psd, then f decreases along the direction where ∇^2 is not psd.)

14

- Adequate Second Class Conditions: $\nabla^2 f$ continued. In an open neighborhood of x^*, $\nabla f (x^*) = 0$, $\nabla^2 f (x^*)$ pd $\Rightarrow x^*$ is the strict local miniature of f. (Unnecessary condition, for example: $f (x) = x^4$ at $x^* = 0$.) (See: Taylor-expand f about x^*.)

The key to the conditions is that ∇, ∇^2 are present and continuous. The smoothness of f allows us to roughly predict landscapes around the point x.

Convex optimization

- $S \subset R^n$ is a convex set if x, y $\in$ S $\Rightarrow \alpha x + (1 - \alpha) y \in$ S, $\forall \alpha \in$ [0, 1].

- f: $S \subset R^n \rightarrow R$ is a convex function if its field S is convex and $f (\alpha x + (1 - \alpha) y) \leq \alpha f (x) + (1 - \alpha) f (y)$, $\forall \alpha \in$ (0, 1), $\forall$ x, y $\in$ S. Accurately convex: "<" instead of "≤". f is concave (strictly) if −f is convex (strictly).

- Convex optimization problem: objective and meaningful group are both convex ($\Leftarrow$ linear equality constraints and concave inequality constraints). Example: linear programming (LP).

An easier solution because every local minute is a global minute.

2.1 Optimization Models

Models are smaller structures that are used extensively in basic sciences and engineering, reflecting all the features of a large-scale system. Models usually contain details that reflect the basic features of the system and include the intended use of the model. For example, when we drop an airplane that is in the design phase, wind tunnel experiments are carried out using the model of the plane instead of the real plane while examining the aero-dynamic structure of the airplane. In agriculture, while examining all the features of a plant and improving the yield of the plant, the models of the plant are evaluated in the laboratory environment according to different parameters and the results are analyzed.

Optimization models consist of mathematical expressions that reflect the functioning and properties of the system and include interactions with other systems in and around the system. As seen below, these mathematical expressions consist of parameters that determine the measurable features of the system, variables that determine the decision values that will give the best results, the performance criteria to be optimized, and constraints that determine the features and limits of the system:

16

$$\max z = f(x,y)$$
$$\text{k.s. } g(x, y) = 0 \qquad\qquad (1)$$
$$h(x, y) \leq 0$$
$$n \in R^n$$
$$y\{, , ,....,m\}$$

In the optimization problem above, the performance criterion (goal function) of the system is expressed with z = f (x, y) and it is aimed to find the values of decision variables x and y that will maximize this criterion. The properties of the system determine g (x, y) equality and h (x, y) inequalities (constraints). In addition, decision variables are expressed in two ways: continuous variables (x) that can take any real value in n dimensional space and integer variables (y) that can take any integer value. It is classified as follows when the system parameters take the known fixed values according to the characteristics of the decision variables, purpose function and system constraints in which they include optimization models. If y variables are not included in an optimization problem and f (x), g (x) and h (x) functions are linear, that problem is defined as a linear programming problem. If y variables are not included in an optimization problem and any of the functions f (x), g (x) and h (x) are not linear, this problem is a nonlinear programming problem. If there are y variables in optimization problems, if f (x, y), g (x, y) and h (x, y) functions are linear, the problem is integer mixed linear programming problem, f (x, y), g (x, y) and if any

17

of the functions h (x, y) is not linear, integer mixed nonlinear programming is obtained.

2.1.1 Linear Programming Models

In these problems, there are only linear variables and linear constraints with linear purpose function.

$$\begin{aligned} \max z &= c^T x \\ \text{k.s.} \quad Ax &\leq b \\ x &\geq 0 \end{aligned} \quad (2)$$

Linear programming models are the most widely used optimization models and have been widely used in the modeling of scientific, industrial and economic problems. In this context, a simple linear programming model related to optimization of productivity in a manufacturing enterprise is given below.

It is possible to produce two new products in two different factories in a business. The data valid for this business are given in Table 2.1. The time available for the production of new products in both plants is limited. Since the structures of the factories are different, there are different production times for the unit product. In addition, the profit margin and demand of each product is also determined.

	Unit spent for product production time		Total production time available
	Product 1	Product 2	
Factory 1	1	1	100
Factory 2	2	1.5	170
Profit margin	1000	900	
Request	100	100	

Table 2.1. Data for example problems.

The product distribution that maximizes profit in this business can be modeled as follows:

Decision Variables:
- x_1: Production quantity of product 1 (pcs)
- x_2: Production quantity of product 2 (pcs)

Parameters:
- c_1: Profit from product 1 (1.000 TL / piece)
- c_2: Profit amount from product 2 (900 TL / piece)
- b_i: Total available production time in factory 1 (100 hours)
- b_{ii}: Total available production time in factory 1 (170 hours)
- a_{i1}: Production time of Product 1 at Factory 1 (1 hour / piece)
- a_{i2}: Production time of Product 2 at Factory 1 (1 hour / piece)
- a_{ii1}: Production time of Product 1 at Factory 2 (2 hours / piece)
- a_{ii2}: Production time of Product 2 at Factory 2 (1.5 hours / piece)
- d_1: The quantity demanded for product 1 (100 pieces)
- d_2: Demand quantity determined for product 2 (100 items)

Purpose Function:
- Karın Total abdominal maximization ($z = c1x1 + c2x2$)

Constraints:

- Toplam Total production time in factory 1 is limited ($a_{i1}x_1 + a_{i2}x_2 \leq b_i$)
- Toplam Total production time in factory 2 is limited ($a_{ii1}x_1 + a_{ii2}x_2 \leq b_i$)
- Talep Demand quantity for product 1 ($x_1 \leq d_1$)
- Talep Demand quantity for product 2 ($x_2 \leq d_2$)
- En Lowest production quantity for each product ($x_1 \geq 0$ and $x_2 \geq 0$)
The linear programming model for this problem is created as

follows:

$$\max z = 1000x_1 + 900x_2$$
$$\text{K.s.} \qquad 1x_1 + 1x_2$$
$$\leq 100$$
$$2x_1 + 1.5x_2$$
$$\leq 170$$
$$x_1$$
$$\leq 100$$
$$2x_2$$
$$\leq 100$$
$$x_1 \geq 0,$$
$$x_2 \geq 0$$

2.1.2 Integer-Mixed Linear Programming Models

In these models, in addition to the linear programming features, some of the decision variables can only take integer values.

$$\max z = c^T x \, d_T y$$
$$\text{k.s.} \qquad Ax \, Ey \leq b$$
$$x \geq 0$$
$$y \in \{0,1,2,...,n$$
$$\}$$

Let's assume that we can choose only one of the two products in the linear programming model given above. If we choose the first product, we need to make 1,500 TL for once, so that we can make the necessary arrangements in the factories, and the second product requires 1,200 TL. We need to add the following to the linear programming model:

Decision Variables:
- y_1 = first product selection (= 1 if first product is selected, = 0 if first product is not selected)
- y_2 = second product selection (= 1 if second product is selected, = 0 if second product is not selected).

Parameters:
- e_1: the cost to be made when the first product is selected (1.500 TL)
- e_2: the cost to be made when the second product is selected (1.200 TL)

Purpose Function:
- Total profit maximization ($z = c_1x_1 + c_2x_2 - e_1x_1 - e_2x_2$)

Constraints:
- Only one product can be selected ($y_1 + y_2 = 1$)

Linear programming model (5) for this problem:

$$\max\ z = 1.000x_1 + 900x_2 - 1.500y_1 - 1.200y_2$$

$$
\begin{aligned}
\text{k.s.} \quad & x_1 + && x_2 && && \leq 100 \\
& 2x_1 + && 1{,}5x_2 && && \leq 170 \\
& x_1 && && -100y_1 && \leq 0 \\
& && x_2 && && -100y_2 \leq 0 \\
& && && y_1 + && y_2 = 1
\end{aligned}
$$

$$x_1 \geq 0, \quad x_2 \geq 0, \quad y_1 \in \{0,1\}, y_2 \in \{0,1\}$$

2.1.3 Nonlinear Programming Models

In these models, some of the objective function and / or constraints are not linear. As a result of optimization, decision variables that will optimize the objective function can take any real value in x, n dimensional space.

$$
\begin{aligned}
\max\ z &= f(x) \\
\text{k.s.} \quad & g(x) = 0 \\
& h(x) \leq 0 \\
& x \in R^n
\end{aligned}
$$

In our linear programming example model, let's assume that the snow we will obtain for each acre is elastic: the more we use our agricultural land for a product, the amount of profit we get from each acre is decreasing. In this case, unit profit amounts, c1 and c2, are expressed as in (7):

$$c_1 = \frac{1.000}{(x_1)^{1/E_1}}, \quad c_2 = \frac{900}{(x_2)^{1/E_2}} \tag{7}$$

In these expressions, E1 and E2 represent snow elasticity. In our example problem, when this value is 15 for the first product and 10 for the second product, the nonlinear optimization problem occurs as given in (8):

$$\max \ z = \frac{1.000}{(x_1)^{1/15}} x_1 + \frac{900}{(x_2)^{1/10}} x_2$$

$$\begin{aligned}
\text{k.s.} \quad x_1 + & \quad x_2 \leq 100 \\
2x_1 + & \quad 1{,}5x_2 \leq 170 \\
x_1 + & \quad \leq 100 \\
& \quad x_2 \leq 100 \\
x_1 \geq 0, & \quad x_2 \geq 0
\end{aligned} \tag{8}$$

2.1.4   Integer-Mixed Nonlinear Programming Models

These models include nonlinear expressions and integer variables in the goal function and / or constraints. The general version of these models is given at the beginning of this section. In our example problem, if there is profit flexibility and we need to choose only one of the two products, the optimization model is as follows:

23

$$\max z = \frac{1.000}{(x_1)^{1/15}} x_1 + \frac{900}{(x_2)^{1/10}} x_2 - 1.500 y_1 - 1.200 y_2$$

$$
\begin{array}{llll}
\text{k.s.} & x_1 + & x_2 & \leq 100 \\
& 2x_1 + & 1,5x_2 & \leq 170 \\
& x_1 & -100 y_1 & \leq 0 \\
& & x_2 \qquad -100 y_2 & \leq 0 \\
& & y_1 + \quad y_2 = 1 \\
& x_1 \geq 0, & x_2 \geq 0, \quad y_1 \in \{0,1\}, \; y_2 \in \{0,1\}
\end{array}
$$

(9)

2.2 Linear Programming

Linear Program (LP)

o Linear objective function, linear restrictions (equality + inequality); Possible combination: polytope (= convex; flat-sided group); Objective function features: Airplanes. The solution: Either none (the meaningful set is empty or the problem is unlimited), one (vertex) or infinite number (edge, face, etc.).

o Standard Model LP: $\min_x c^T x$ s.t. $Ax = b$; $x \geq 0$, where c, x R^n, b $\in R^m$, $A_{m \times n}$. Assume that m <n and A have a full row arrangement (otherwise $Ax = b$ contains redundant or unenforceable rows or specifies a unique point).

o Standardization techniques (generally applicable after LP):

- max $c^T x$ − −min $(-c)^T x$.

- infinite variable x: division of x into non-negative and non-positive parts: $x = x^+ - x^-$ where $x^+ = \max(x, 0) \geq 0$ and $x^- = \max(-x, 0) \geq 0$. ($x^+ x^- = 0$)

- $Ax \leq b$: add slack variables $\Leftrightarrow Ax + y = b$, $y \geq 0$.

- $Ax \geq b$: add the surplus variables $\Leftrightarrow Ax - y = b$, $y \geq 0$.

Example:

$$\min \ c^T x \text{ s.t. } Ax \geq b \ \Leftrightarrow \ \min \left(\begin{smallmatrix} c \\ -c \\ 0 \end{smallmatrix} \right)^T \left(\begin{smallmatrix} x^+ \\ x^- \\ z \end{smallmatrix} \right) \text{ s.t. } (A \ -A \ -I) \left(\begin{smallmatrix} x^+ \\ x^- \\ z \end{smallmatrix} \right) = b, \ \left(\begin{smallmatrix} x^+ \\ x^- \\ z \end{smallmatrix} \right) \geq 0.$$

• LP is a very special case of restricted improvements, but is common due to its simplicity and program availability.

• LP commercial programs are accepted as standard.

2.2.1 Optimality conditions

LP is a convex optimization problem - i.e. a microsd is a universal microsd; KKT conditions are necessary and sufficient as well; LICQ not necessary? KKT conditions:

$$\underbrace{\mathcal{L}(x, \lambda, s)}_{\text{Lagrange multipliers}} = c^T x - \lambda^T (Ax - b) - s^T x. \text{ If x is a solution} \Rightarrow \exists! \ \lambda \in \mathbb{R}^m, \ s \in \mathbb{R}^n:$$

Lagrange multipliers

$$\left.\begin{array}{ll} \text{a)} & A^T \lambda + s = c \\ \text{b)} & Ax = b \\ \text{c)} & x \geq 0 \\ \text{d)} & s \geq 0 \\ \text{e)} & x_i s_i = 0, \ i = 1, \ldots, n \Leftrightarrow x^T s = 0 \end{array}\right\} \Rightarrow c^T x \overset{\text{a)}}{=} (A^T \lambda + s)^T x = (Ax)^T \lambda \overset{\text{b)}}{=} b^T \lambda.$$

KKT conditions are also sufficient. Pf .: Let $\bar{x}$ be another possible point $\Leftrightarrow A\bar{x} = b$, $\bar{x} \geq 0$. Then $c^T\bar{x}_{a)} = (A^T \lambda + s)^T \bar{x} = b^T \lambda + \bar{x}^T s \underset{\bar{x}, s \geq 0}{\overset{\geq}{}} b^T \lambda = c^T x$. The optimal $\bar{x} \Leftrightarrow \bar{x}^T s = 0$.

2.2.2 Dual problem

• Primal problem: min $c^T x$ s.t. $Ax = b$, $x \geq 0$.

Dual problem: max $b^T \lambda$ s.t. $A^T \lambda \leq c$, or min $- b^T \lambda$ s.t. $c -$

$A^T \lambda \geq 0$

x: primal variables (n), λ: dual variables (m).

• KKT conditions for the dual: $L(\lambda, x) = \lambda b^T \lambda - x^T (c - A^T \lambda)$.

If λ is a solution $\Rightarrow \exists! x$:

$Ax = b$
$A^T\_ \leq c$
$x \geq 0$
$x_i (c - A^T \lambda)_i = 0$, $i = 1, \ldots, n$

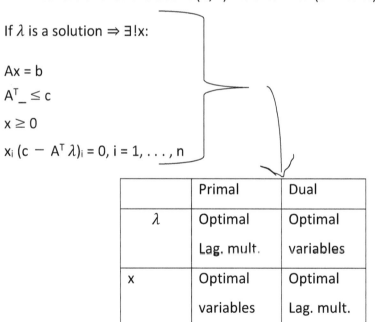

	Primal	Dual
λ	Optimal Lag. mult.	Optimal variables
x	Optimal variables	Optimal Lag. mult.

Which matches the KKT conditions for the underlying problem if we specify s = c - Aᵀ λ,

• Dual = Basic. Pf.: Dual repositioning in the standard LP format by entering stagnation variables s ≥ 0 (so that Aᵀ + s = c) and dividing the unrestricted variables λ into λ = λ⁺ - λ⁻ with λ⁺, λ⁻ ≥ 0. Then we can write the binary as follows:

$$\min \begin{pmatrix} -b \\ b \\ 0 \end{pmatrix}^T \begin{pmatrix} \lambda^+ \\ \lambda^- \\ s \end{pmatrix} \text{ s.t. } (A^T - A^T \ I) \begin{pmatrix} \lambda^+ \\ \lambda^- \\ s \end{pmatrix} = c, \ \begin{pmatrix} \lambda^+ \\ \lambda^- \\ s \end{pmatrix} \geq 0$$

whose dual is

$$\max c^T z \text{ s.t. } \begin{pmatrix} A \\ -A \\ I \end{pmatrix} z \leq \begin{pmatrix} -b \\ b \\ 0 \end{pmatrix} \Leftrightarrow \min -c^T z \text{ s.t. } Az = -b, \ z \leq 0$$

i.e., the primal with z ≡ -x.

• Duplication gap: Looking at the feasible vector x for a primitive (⟺ Ax = b, x ≥ 0) and a possible vector (λ, s) for the duality (⟺ Aᵀ λ + s = c, s ≥ 0) we have:

$$0 \leq x^T s = x^T (c - A^T \lambda) = \underbrace{c^T x - b^T \lambda}_{\text{gap}} \Leftrightarrow c^T x \geq b^T \lambda.$$

27

Thus, the $b^T \lambda$ target function is a lower bound to the primary target function $c^T x$ (weak duplication); Upon solution, the gap is 0.

Strong duplication:

1. If either problem (primitive or dual) has a (finite) solution, then the other, and the objective values are equal.

2. If the problem (primary or dual) is unlimited, the other problem cannot be solved.

Duplication is important in LP theory (and generally convex option) and in dual elementary algorithms; Also, its solution may be easier than primitive.

Sensitivity Analysis: Sensitivity of the global objective value to disturbance disturbances $\Leftrightarrow$ Find multiples of Lagrange λ, s.

2.3 Method of Interpolation Polynomials

Interpolation, which means that there is an unknown $f(\bar{x})$ intermediate value at any $\bar{x}$ intermediate point, starting from the known values of f_i (i = 0,1, ... N) at the x_i (i = 0,1, ... N) points of a function. techniques are also the basis of other numerical methods such as numerical derivatives and integration, numerical solution of ordinary and partial differential equations.

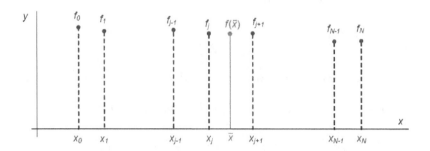

Interpolation methods are usually applied by fitting curves or curves to existing (x_i, f_i) data points. The functions used for this purpose are called interpolation functions.

Various order polynomials are often used as interpolation function. However, in some cases, more specific functions such as logarithmic, exponential, hyperbolic, and trigonometric functions can be used for periodic data values.

Finite difference-based interpolation methods are more suitable if the data points are equally spaced, linear interpolation, Lagrange interpolation, etc. methods are more suitable.

It is possible to pass a polynomial of N degrees from the N + 1 point in the plane. for example

$$P_0\left(\begin{array}{c} x_0 = 3.2 \\ f_0 = 22.0 \end{array}\right). \quad P_1\left(\begin{array}{c} x_1 = 2.7 \\ f_1 = 17.8 \end{array}\right). \quad P_2\left(\begin{array}{c} x_2 = 1.0 \\ f_2 = 14.2 \end{array}\right). \quad P_3\left(\begin{array}{c} x_3 = 4.8 \\ f_3 = 38.3 \end{array}\right). \quad P_4\left(\begin{array}{c} x_4 = 5.6 \\ f_4 = 51.7 \end{array}\right).$$

Let's consider the points. From the first four of these points

$f(x) = a_0 + a_1 x + a_2 x^2 + a_3 x^3$

It is possible to pass a third-order polynomial (cubic). Since the coordinates of each point will provide this equation

$$a_0 + (3.2)a_1 + (3.2)^2 a_2 + (3.2)^3 a_3 = 22.0$$
$$a_0 + (2.7)a_1 + (2.7)^2 a_2 + (2.7)^3 a_3 = 17.8$$
$$a_0 + (1.0)a_1 + (1.0)^2 a_2 + (1.0)^3 a_3 = 14.2$$
$$a_0 + (4.8)a_1 + (4.8)^2 a_2 + (4.8)^3 a_3 = 38.3$$

four equations are obtained. This linear equation set is in matrix form

$$\begin{bmatrix} 1 & 3.2 & 10.24 & 32.768 \\ 1 & 2.7 & 7.29 & 19.683 \\ 1 & 1.0 & 1.00 & 1.000 \\ 1 & 4.8 & 23.04 & 110.592 \end{bmatrix} \begin{bmatrix} a_0 \\ a_1 \\ a_2 \\ a_3 \end{bmatrix} = \begin{Bmatrix} 22.0 \\ 17.8 \\ 14.2 \\ 38.3 \end{Bmatrix}$$

cubic coefficients if they are arranged and solved by Gauss-elimination method, for example.

$a_0 = 24.3499$; $a_1 = -16.1177$; $a_2 = 6.4952$; $a_0 = -0.5275$

It is found as. So the interpolation function

$$f(x) = 24.3496 - 16.1176 x + 6.4952x^2 - 0.5275x^3$$

It shaped. Accordingly, $y = 20.212$ is obtained for the intermediate value at $x = 3.0$ for example. If the last four of the data values are used instead of the first four, the intermediate value at the same point will probably be somewhat different.

2.3.1 Linear interpolation

Instead of solving a set of linear equations as above, to make interpolation by passing a polynomial from a group of points, it is possible to put the resulting formulas into a form suitable for direct interpolation by making appropriate arrangements. For example (x_0, f_0) and (x_1, f_1) two points such as $f(x) = a_0 + a_1 x$

If it is desired to make an interpolation according to the above method by passing a line, the point coordinates will provide the correct equation.

$$F_0 = a_0 + a_1 x_0$$

$$F_1 = a_0 + a_1 x_0$$

Two equations such as are obtained. By solving this system of equations for coefficients

$$a_0 = \frac{f_0 x_1 - f_1 x_0}{x_1 - x_0}; \ a_1 = \frac{f_1 - f_0}{x_1 - x_0}$$

obtained. So the right equation

$$f(x) = \frac{f_0 x_1 - f_1 x_0}{x_1 - x_0} + \frac{f_1 - f_0}{x_1 - x_0}$$

comes to shape. By editing this equation for f_0 and f_1

$$f(x) = L_0 f_0 + L_1 f_1 \qquad L_0 = \frac{x - x_1}{x_0 - x_1}; \ L_1 = \frac{x - x_0}{x_1 - x_0} \qquad \text{it}$$

can also be written.

2.3.2 Lagrange polynomials

If (x_0, f_0), (x_1, f_1) and (x_2, f_2) from three points, $f(x) = a_0 + a_1 x + a_2 x^2$

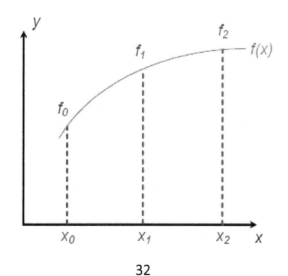

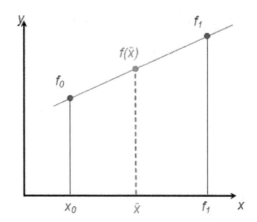

If it is desired to make an interpolation by passing a parabola, this time with the help of point coordinates

$$F_0 = a_0 + a_1 x_0 + a_2 x_0^2$$

$$F_1 = a_0 + a_1 x_1 + a_2 x_1^2$$

$$F_2 = a_0 + a_1 x_2 + a_2 x_2^2$$

the system of equations is obtained, the coefficients of the solution of this system of equations

$$a_0 = \frac{f_0\left(x_1 x_2^2 - x_2 x_1^2\right) + f_1\left(x_2 x_0^2 - x_0 x_2^2\right) + f_2\left(x_0 x_1^2 - x_1 x_0^2\right)}{\left(x_0 - x_1\right)\left(x_0 - x_2\right)\left(x_2 - x_1\right)}$$

$$a_1 = \frac{f_0\left(x_1^2 - x_2^2\right) + f_1\left(x_2^2 - x_0^2\right) + f_2\left(x_0^2 - x_1^2\right)}{\left(x_0 - x_1\right)\left(x_0 - x_2\right)\left(x_2 - x_1\right)}$$

$$a_2 = \frac{f_0\left(x_2 - x_0\right) + f_1\left(x_0 - x_2\right) + f_2\left(x_1 - x_0\right)}{\left(x_0 - x_1\right)\left(x_0 - x_2\right)\left(x_2 - x_1\right)}$$

33

It is found as. In this case, the parabola equation is edited for

f_0, f_1 and f_2. $f(x) = L_0 f_0 + L_1 f_1 + L_2 f_2$

in a simpler form. L_i sizes here

$$L_0 = \frac{(x-x_1)(x-x_2)}{(x_0-x_1)(x_0-x_2)}; \qquad L_1 = \frac{(x-x_0)(x-x_2)}{(x_1-x_0)(x_1-x_2)}; \qquad L_2 = \frac{(x-x_0)(x-x_1)}{(x_2-x_0)(x_2-x_1)}$$

These sizes are called Lagrange polynomials. For higher degree curves based on these two examples;

$$f(x) = \sum_{k=0}^{N} L_k f_k$$

It is possible to make a generalization. The Lagrange polynomial here is based on the examples above;

$$L_k = \frac{(x-x_0)(x-x_1)\ldots\ldots(x-x_{k-1})(x-x_{k+1})\ldots\ldots(x-x_N)}{(x_k-x_0)(x_k-x_1)\ldots\ldots(x_k-x_{k-1})(x_k-x_{k+1})\ldots\ldots(x_k-x_N)} = \prod_{\substack{j=0 \\ j\neq k}}^{N} \frac{x-x_j}{x_k-x_j}$$

It can be written as.

Example:

Let the values of an $f(x)$ function at the points $x = 0,1,2$ be given as $f = 1,2,4$, respectively. Lagrange functions if $N = 2$

$$L_0 = \frac{(x-1)(x-2)}{(0-1)(0-2)}; \quad L_1 = \frac{(x-0)(x-2)}{(1-0)(1-2)}; \quad L_2$$
$$= \frac{(x-0)(x-1)}{(2-0)(2-1)}$$

can be calculated as. In this case, the interpolation function

$$f(x) = \frac{(x-1)(x-2)}{2} x1 + \frac{(x-0)(x-2)}{(-1)} x2$$

$$+ \frac{(x-0)(x-1)}{2} x4$$

if this function is arranged for x

$$f(x) = \frac{1}{2}x^2 + \frac{1}{2}x + 1$$

It can be made into shape. The same function, N = 2nd order polynomial

$$f(x) = a_0 + a_1 x + a_2 x^2$$

and will be written with the help of data points

$1 = a_0 + a_1\, 0 + a_2\, 0$

$2 = a_0 + a_1\, 1 + a_2\, 1$

$4 = a_0 + a_1\, 2 + a_2\, 4$

It is also possible to obtain by solving the set of linear equations.

Warning

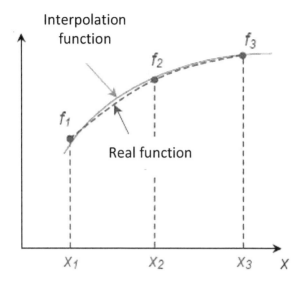

Curves fitting to a data distribution, that is, the interpolation functions used are often different from the actual function that produces the data points. In this regard, it is very important to select the interpolation function accurately.

For example, if the polynomic approaches described above are used for interpolation, if the degree of the polynomial is selected less than necessary, an error occurs in the interpolation value. If the value of the polynomial is chosen larger than necessary, unexpected and unfavourable fluctuations occur in the interpolation function. Interpolation value is again obtained incorrectly.

2.3.3 Neville Method

Neville method is a different application of Lagrange method in closed form and it is expected to eliminate the weaknesses of Lagrange method.

In this method, the interpolation value is calculated by increasing the degree of the polynomial. Each time the value of the polynomial is increased, it is checked whether the interpolation value obtained converges with the previous value.

Let's assume that the values of a function are given as (f_0, f_1, f_2) in three data points such as (x_0, x_1, x_2) as an example for the method to be well understood.

If there is a linear interpolation between the first two points, Lagrange formula

$$f(x) = \frac{x - x_1}{x_0 - x_1} f_0 + \frac{x - x_0}{x_1 - x_0} f_1$$

It can be written as. This time for Lagrange formula if linear interpolation is done between the last two points.

$$f(x) = \frac{x - x_2}{x_1 - x_2} f_1 + \frac{x - x_1}{x_2 - x_1} f_2$$

obtained.

Lagrange formula if interpolated by passing a parabolic curve between three points

$$f(x) = \frac{(x - x_1)(x - x_2)}{(x_0 - x_1)(x_0 - x_2)} f_0 + \frac{(x - x_0)(x - x_2)}{(x_1 - x_0)(x_1 - x_2)} f_1$$
$$+ \frac{(x - x_0)(x - x_1)}{(x_2 - x_0)(x_2 - x_1)} f_2$$

It can be written as. Coefficient of the second term in this formula

$$\frac{(x-x_0)(x-x_2)}{(x_1-x_0)(x_1-x_2)} = \frac{(x-x_0)(x-x_2)}{(x_1-x_0)(x_1-x_2)} \cdot \frac{(x_0-x_2)}{(x_0-x_2)} = \frac{(x-x_0)(x-x_2)}{(x_0-x_2)} \cdot \frac{(x_0-x_2)}{(x_1-x_0)(x_1-x_2)}$$
$$= \frac{(x-x_0)(x-x_2)}{(x_0-x_2)} \cdot \left[\frac{1}{(x_1-x_0)} - \frac{1}{(x_1-x_2)} \right]$$
$$= \frac{(x-x_0)(x-x_2)}{(x_0-x_2)(x_1-x_0)} + \frac{(x-x_0)(x-x_2)}{(x_2-x_0)(x_1-x_2)}$$

arranged in the form of Lagrange formula

$$f(x) = \frac{(x-x_1)(x-x_2)}{(x_0-x_1)(x_0-x_2)} f_0 + \frac{(x-x_0)(x-x_2)}{(x_0-x_2)(x_1-x_0)} f_1 + \frac{(x-x_0)(x-x_2)}{(x_2-x_0)(x_1-x_2)} f_1 + \frac{(x-x_0)(x-x_1)}{(x_2-x_0)(x_2-x_1)} f_2$$

It can be made into shape. This formula

$$f(x) = \frac{(x-x_2)}{(x_0-x_2)} \left[\frac{(x-x_1)}{(x_0-x_1)} f_0 + \frac{(x-x_0)}{(x_1-x_0)} f_1 \right] + \frac{(x-x_0)}{(x_2-x_0)} \left[\frac{(x-x_2)}{(x_1-x_2)} f_1 + \frac{(x-x_1)}{(x_2-x_1)} f_2 \right]$$

It is possible to edit. It is noteworthy that the terms contained in square brackets here are the values found by previous linear interpolation. According to this:

Function values at data points $P_{00} = f_0$; $P_{10} = f_1$; $P_{20} = f_2$ And the values found with the first linear interpolation

$$P_{01} = \frac{x - x_1}{x_0 - x_1} P_{00} + \frac{x - x_0}{x_1 - x_0} P_{10} \qquad P_{11}$$

$$= \frac{x - x_2}{x_1 - x_2} P_{10} + \frac{x - x_1}{x_2 - x_1} P_{20}$$

If it is renamed as, the last formula obtained as a result of the parabolic approach is also briefly

$$P_{02} = \frac{(x - x_2)}{(x_0 - x_2)} P_{01} + \frac{(x - x_0)}{(x_2 - x_0)} P_{11}$$

It can be arranged as. This statement consists of a new linear interpolation between the values found with the first linear interpolations, as is clearly seen.

As a result, the Lagrange formula written for linear interpolation constitutes the basis of the Neville method. To increase the degree of the Lagrange polynomial, a new linear interpolation is made between the interpolation values found in the previous degree.

Example:

With the help of the data points on the side, you want to find the interpolation value at x = 27.5.

x	f(x)
10.1	0.17537
22.2	0.37784
32.0	0.52992
41.6	0.66393
50.5	0.63608

First, let's sort the points according to their distance from the interpolation point:

i	x-x_i	x_i	f(x)
0	4.5	32.0	0.52992
1	5.3	22.2	0.37784
2	14.1	41.6	0.66393
3	17.4	10.1	0.17537
4	23.0	50.5	0.63608

By applying consecutive linear interpolations as explained above, it is possible to obtain a table as follows:

i	x-x_i	x_i	P_{i0}	P_{i1}	P_{i2}	P_{i3}	P_{i4}
0	4.5	32.0	0.52992	0.46009	0.46200	0.46174	0.45754
1	5.3	22.2	0.37784	0.45600	0.46071	0.47901	
2	14.1	41.6	0.66393	0.44524	0.55843		
3	17.4	10.1	0.17537	0.37329			
4	23.0	50.5	0.63608				

40

Here, the top row contains the interpolation values to be obtained with Lagrange formulas of various degrees at the interpolation point. It is noteworthy that the interpolation value converges to a certain value from the 3rd degree to a Langrange formulation, but divergence occurs in the interpolation value if the fourth-order Lagrange formula is used. It is understood, therefore, that at this interpolation point, the 3rd order approach is sufficient for calculation. As a matter of fact, the values given in this example are the values of the sine function versus angles in degrees and the real value of the sine function at the interpolation point $x =$ 27.5 is sin (27.5 °) = 0.46175.

Computer vision is to detect objects using optical tools and gather information accordingly or manage various processes without any physical interaction with the environment. Within this definition, computer vision should naturally be in cooperation with many different branches of science. As an example, let's take the 3D picture of an object seen from the camera, which is one of the most classic computer vision problems. In such a system, the following disciplines will be needed,

• Mechanical engineering: A device design that moves the camera or the object so that it can show the object properly to the camera.

• Optical engineering: Various optical methods can be used to improve image quality from the camera.

• Camera technology: Cameras vary widely. These include sensitivity, resolution, weight, resistance to electrical noise, vibration, magnetic waves, radiation, durability, projection shape (perspective, linear).

• Signal processing hardware: Camcorders often produce enough information to compel the processing capacity of computers, so specialized hardware will be needed.

• Artificial Intelligence: Algorithms of software that will make pattern recog-nition that will define the data and expert systems to make decisions (Expert Systems) must be implemented.

• Software Engineering: You will need software to process complex data such as detected data and make decisions.

• Mathematics: Extracting 3-dimensional objects from 2D images and processing them will require high levels of mathematics. This is of particular interest to electronics Engineering.

Concepts:

Seeing, Appearance and Image: The perception of objects by reflecting the rays that hit their surface or passing through them, seeing. The two-dimensional (2-D) image of the view obtained in any form is called the image. The image can also be defined as the map of the three-dimensional (3-D) view on two dimensions.

Image: Visual representations, each of which contains position information $f(x, y)$ and color information, are all images. These pictures can be handled in two parts as analog and digital image.

Analog image: If the analog image (f (x, y)), which forms the function in a certain range of max and min, takes real values (including decimal values) that change constantly, this image is Analog image. No matter how closely we look at an image in an analog image (for example, with a microscope), there are still the colors that make up the image. Digital computers cannot process continuous functions / parameters. These functions need to be digitized.

Digital (Digital) image: Continuous image (analog image) represented as f (x, y) is expressed in discrete samples and its representation is f [x, y].

Pixel: Each element of a digital image in the form of a 2-dimensional array f [x, y] is called a pixel or pel ("image element"). The figure below shows the same picture with different pixels.

200x200   100x100   50x50   25x25

3.1 Light

What is light, the light is an energy. There are several theories about light. Light has been proven to be both matter (mass) and energy (wave). Light is small wavelets emitted by the light source. These wavelets are in the form of radiation energy (electromagnetic radiation). It spreads around in straight lines. The visible light is in a very small range in the electromagnetic spectrum (around 2%). We cannot see light waves outside this range with the naked eye.

Each color in the visible light region has a wavelength. Generally, the wavelength of the light we see with our eyes is in the range of 0.380-0.760 microns (370 -760 nanometers). If we take the speed of light 300 thousand km per second, we can find its frequency from the link below. According to this connection, light can be expressed in both frequency (v) and wavelength (λ).

c (Speed of light) = v (frequency) * λ (wavelength)

If the white light is decomposed into its own colors, it is seen that it consists of a color band (spectrum). As the wavelength of light advances from small value to large value, its color changes from blue (purple) to red (scarlet).

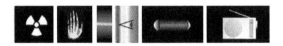

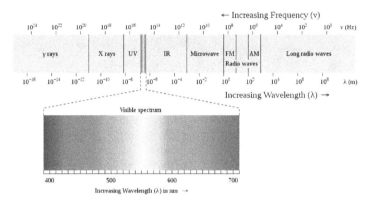

Figure 3.1. Electromagnetic spectrum.

New colors can be obtained by mixing certain colors with each other. For example, in vehicles with display, three colors are used with RGB code (Red, Green, Blue) and different color mixtures of these colors with certain brightness are obtained.

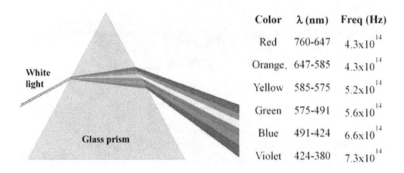

Color	λ (nm)	Freq (Hz)
Red	760-647	4.3×10^{14}
Orange.	647-585	4.3×10^{14}
Yellow	585-575	5.2×10^{14}
Green	575-491	5.6×10^{14}
Blue	491-424	6.6×10^{14}
Violet	424-380	7.3×10^{14}

Figure 3.2. Color Spectrum.

The speed of light is 299.792.458 m / s (300.000 km / h) in the vacuum. In the MKS unit system, the wavelength unit is meters (m) and the frequency unit is Hertz (Hz).

An all-black body is completely invisible, such as ultraviolet (ultraviolet) and infrared (infrared-infrared) rays. It absorbs all the light that falls on it. However, when the object is heated, it only emits limited and specific colors and frequencies. Infrared rays are emitted first. Then as it warms up, it becomes red and as a result white. If it could be heated enough, it would turn blue and radiate ultraviolet rays like the hottest stars.

There are some benefits to changing the frequency of light or making the invisible frequency visible. Fluorescent substances (phosphorous) receive light at different frequencies and emit them at different frequencies. As the

47

lights sent to him make the lights that we cannot see, their reflections become brighter. This is the basis of the paints and inks used in some advertisements. Some cleaning powders contain optical brighteners that convert invisible ultraviolet rays to blue light, making the garment brighter. The light used in the control of the coins is also not visible to the light reflected on the money, but it shines while reflecting back to such special paints on the money.

In addition, the system in night vision cameras brings the infrared (hot) rays that we cannot see to the eye to the wavelength that we can see and make them appear.

3.2   Image Processing

Image processing algorithms are the most integral part of computer vision systems working in many disciplines. These algorithms can be examined in 3 different categories as input and output.

image processing: image -> output: image

image analysis input: image -> output: measurements

Image Understanding input: image -> output: definition

3.2.1 2D viewing

The image can be modeled with a 2 dimensional n * m matrix. Each element of this matrix determines the intensity of that pixel between black and white. The values of pixels in bits and the dimensions of the image in horizontal and vertical pixels affect the quality and size of the image. In an 8-bit black and white image, if a pixel is O, it is "black", 255 is "white". They take black and white values proportionally between the values.

Let's give an example to understand the images better. If it is 200 * 200 size and 8 bits are used for each pixel. 200 * 200 * 8/8 (number of bits / number of bits per one byte) = 40000 bytes = covers an area of 40 kilobytes. This information is true if the image is stored as a binary map (bitmap). There are various compressed image formats that can reduce the size of these files.

The display of color images is slightly different. Although there are different display formats, the most common is RGB [Red (Red), Blue (Blue), Green (Green)] display. This representation assumes that each color can be created with a mixture of these three colors. Mathematically, for these three colors, individual matrices can be considered.

In an image processing algorithm, its input is an image output and another image, three kinds of different situations can be observed.

1. Coordinate at one point of the output depends on the same cone of the input.

2. The cone at one point of the output depends on the neighboring coats of the same cone of the input.

3. The cone at one point of the output depends on each pixel value in the input.

3.2.2   3D viewing

The easiest way to display three-dimensional images is probably the images that are kept as "depth map". The difference of these images from 2D gray level images is that they contain depth level information instead of gray level information.

3.2.3   Fourier Methods

Fourier transforms are an important method used in signal processing. Each signal is basically formed by the combination of a signal at a certain frequency and its frequency as well as the linear combination of different signals at different rates. For example, let's consider a one-dimensional signal (sound, for example). This signal will consist of different periodic signals with frequencies such as f, 2f, 3f... nf. The coefficients of these signals will give us a significant clue about the character of the signal. Digital audio is obtained by sampling a one-dimensional analog signal (For example, 8000 per second). Then this signal approximation is divided into windows of 20 ms, and the Fourier transform of each is taken and as a result, a graphic called spectogram that gives the general characteristic of the sound is obtained.

The images are formed as a result of sampling an analog signal such as sound, so it should not be surprised to use the techniques used in sound analysis, the only difference of the image is that it is a 2D signal.

So, what does the frequency of the picture mean? If the frequencies in a picture are high, there are rapid changes in the picture. If the frequency is generally low, then entropy is a low image.

Fourier methods are defined for continuous functions, but the information in the images is numerical and discrete. DFT (Discrete Fourier Transfrom) is used for these. DFT is a time consuming algorithm if used directly, but if the problem is broken down, it can be calculated very quickly, which is the basis of the FFT (Fast Fourier Transform) algorithm.

3.2.4   Softening images in Fourier Space

Noise in an image usually means sudden ups and downs in images, which correspond to high frequency components. If we pass our image through a frequency filter and do not allow high frequencies, we naturally reduce the effect of a noise.

3.2.5   softening images in real space

The easiest method of image softening in real space is to average a pixel relative to surrounding pixels.

3.2.6   Edge Detection

Defining edges has an important place in image processing. The reasons for this are that it takes less time to find the edges and gives important clues about the identification of the objects. In 1, an edge difference occurred when the surfaces came side by side.

3.2.7 Defining a gradient based edge tip

One of the methods used to define the ends of the edges is that the slope on the edge makes a discontinuous jump while it is continuous. This is an indication of a corner. There are different types of edging. Some of those :

3.2.8 Edge Blending

Edge identifiers return points on the same line to us. What we need to do next is to combine all these points and turn them into a single line. Also, some of the problems we will encounter are as follows. Small parts of the edge may be lost, the noise in the image may show as if there are edges that are not pictured. In general, edge joining methods are divided into two.

Local Edge Connectors In this type of algorithm, each point looks at its relationship with its neighbor and forms the edge.

General Edge Connectors In such algorithms, all points in the picture are checked at the same time whether they meet a certain similarity criterion or not, like the correct equation.

3.2.9 Local Edge joining methods

Many edge detectors provide information about the direction of the slope at any point on the edge. This information is very useful when creating the edge because the points adjacent to each other will have the same derivative.

Local edge binding methods generally start at a certain point and continue by putting their neighbors into a similarity test. If the dots fit the similarity test, the dots are added to the current edge set.

Then the same process is continued with the newly added points. If any point around the point does not have the edge properties, we are at the end of the edge.

3.2.10 Segmentation

Another way to get information from images is by cutting. Segmentation is used to distinguish the rest of a given area in others.

• 2D: The pixels in the picture are grouped according to the change in their density.

• 3D: The pixels in the picture are displayed according to the rate of change of their depth. Basic cutting patterns are as follows.

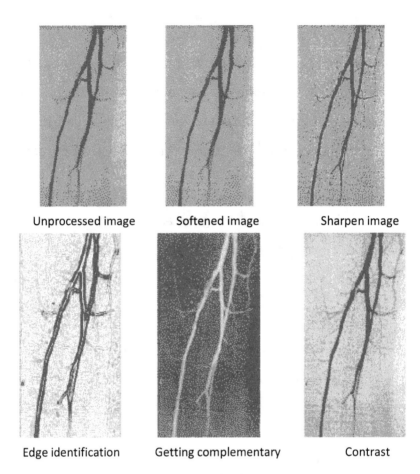

Unprocessed image	Softened image	Sharpen image

Edge identification	Getting complementary	Contrast

3.2.11 Region Splitting

First, the image is considered as a whole. Then the image is checked. If all parts are compatible, the algorithm will end later. If incompatible, the region is divided into 4 main parts and the algorithm continues for each. This process continues until there are no more divisions. It is a divide and conquer tactics. The worst possible result is that everything is split up to the smallest pixel. In order to prevent such consequences, neighbors are looked after after each division, whether an appropriate merger can be made.

3.2.12 Region Growing

Region growth is an algorithm that goes the opposite way of region separation. Small regions are combined as initial values. This is done by finding any starting seed point. When the growth of the region stops, the processes that are not included in any region are selected and the process continues.

3.2.13 Optical Flow

If we take a series of images over time and there are objects moving in the environment, useful information about the image and the moving object can be collected. For example, consider a moving celestial body. By examining the photographs taken at different times, it can be understood which pixel belongs to the object and which does not move. If we can analyze the movements properly, we can answer the following questions.

1. How many moving objects do you have?

2. In which directions are they moving?

3. If not properly, they move to see a certain function

4. How fast are they.

We calculate a function called optical flow from an array of images. For each pixel, V = (u, v) is found, the following values are calculated in this function field. How fast the pixel moves in the picture. At what speed does the pixel move?

3.2.14 Digital image processing

Digital image processing is concerned with converting an analog image into digital format and then processing it with digital computers for various purposes (improvement, repair, classification, compression, understanding and interpretation, etc.). The basic steps are summarized as follows.

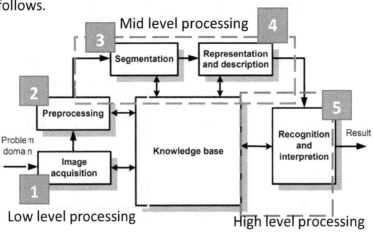

Figure 3.3. Basic steps of digital image processing.

1. Image acquisition: The first step in image processing is the acquisition of digital image by digital camera.

2. Preprocessing: The next step after obtaining digital image is preprocessing. Preprocessing is the preprocessing of the image in order to obtain a more successful result before using the obtained digital image. These operations are basically;

- image enhancement

- image restoration and

- image compression

can be collected under the subheadings. Acquiring and preprocessing the image is called low-level image processing.

3. Segmentation: After pre-processing, partitioning (called segmentation, disassembly, segmentation) step is passed. Segmentation is the most difficult application of image processing, it is the process of separating the object and background in an image or regions with different properties of interest in the image. Partitioning; detects the boundaries and areas of an object in an image, producing raw information on its shape. If we are interested in the shapes of objects, partitioning gives us information about the edges, corners and boundaries of that object. On the other hand, if the internal features of the objects in the image are concerned with their surface coating, area, colors, and skeleton, regional segmentation should be done. Combination of both partitioning methods (boundaries and areas) for the solution of highly complex problems such as character or pattern recognition in general

Required.

4. Representation and description: The raw information obtained from the image, the details of interest are brought to the fore. In other words, it is the separation of the desired special areas from the background and each other.

5. Recognition and interpretion: In this stage, which is included in the high level image processing group, labeling and classification of the objects or regions that are removed from the background in the image with various decision making mechanisms (such as artificial intelligence algorithms).

Operations on digital (digital) image

All of the operations to be performed in the image processing stage are performed on the pixels that make up the image, that is, on the color information that these pixels have. These transactions; point operations can be grouped into three groups: local (regional) operations and holistic operations.

Point Operations: Operations performed on a pixel of the input image to create a pixel of the output image. It is done by changing the color information of the pixel regardless of the neighboring pixels. That is, the operation performed on each pixel in the input image creates the corresponding pixel in the output image.

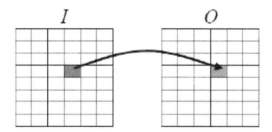

Local Operations: The color of a point that will create the output image here depends on the color characteristics of its neighbors in the entrance image. Which neighbor depends on the color depends on the size of the mask. These masks are shifted on all pixels in the image to filter the image. In this sense; Local processing can be given as an example for eliminating blur, removing noise, and determining edge and region characteristics. In summary, in this process, the value of one pixel in the output image depends on the value of many pixels in the input image.

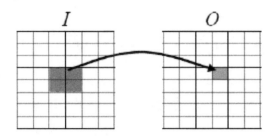

Holistic (global) Transactions: In holistic (global) transactions, the color properties of all pixels of the image affect the pixel of the output image to be rendered. In this process, the value of one pixel in the output image depends on the values of all pixels in the input image.

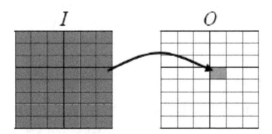

3.2.15 Converting Analog Image to digital

Analog images need to be digitized to be processed in a computer environment. For digitization, sampling is done first and then quantization. In order for the function to be processed in a computer environment, it must be digitized both spatially (spatially) and in amplitude (in color information). While digitizing the coordinates of the image function is called image sampling; Digitization of amplitude values is called image quantization.

Image Sampling:

A numerical image can be created by taking N samples along the x-axis and M samples along its x-axis at equal intervals via a continuous image function. Thus, the transition from the continuous-time image function to the discrete-time image function occurs. An analog image can be expressed approximately by the total N × M finite sample value consisting of N horizontally and M vertical samples in 2-D discrete time. In this process, the analog image function is properly sampled. That is, proper sampling is created by taking samples from the analog image at equal intervals in both horizontal and vertical directions. The resulting digital (digital) image is actually a matrix of N rows and M columns. There is a loss of information in this process.

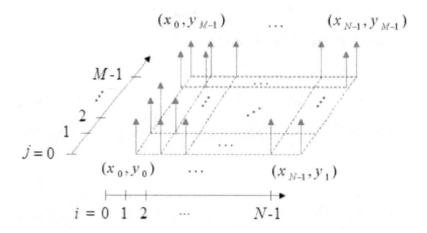

(x_0, y_{M-1}) ... (x_{N-1}, y_{M-1})

$M-1$

2

1

$j = 0$

(x_0, y_0) ... (x_{N-1}, y_1)

$i = 0 \ 1 \ 2$ ... $N-1$

Image Quantization:

The positive integer value of the image, which indicates the brightness intensity of each element (pixel), is determined by quantization. The smallest and largest amplitude values range of the image element is divided into digits and takes the image value closest to the relevant digit value.

As a result of these two operations, a digital image that can be processed by computers is obtained. One of the sample devices that digitizes an analog image by performing both these operations is the scanner. Images obtained in certain formats from the browser are digital and can be processed with software on the computer.

The numerical image obtained after sampling and quantization is in a two-dimensional matrix structure, its

63

components consisting of positive integer values. Each element of the matrix that represents the digital image is called pixels. Pixel is the smallest element that creates a digital image, and the value of a pixel indicates the brightness intensity of the related image element. The positive integer value related to the luminance intensity is determined by quantization.

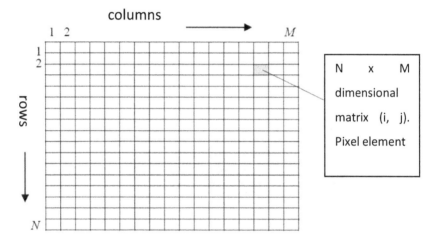

Gray Image:

In the digitization process, it is necessary to determine the image dimensions and the brightness value that each pixel can have. The brightness value of each pixel of the digital image is called gray levels. The gray level range is determined by the number of bits in which the brightness value in each pixel is encoded.

64

There are two colors at the border of your gray level, black and white. The images coded between these two are called gray scale (monochromatic) images.

Each pixel commonly used in the application is encoded with 8 bits. In such images, each pixel consists of 28 = 256 different gray scale equivalent (brightness level) values and the gray value range is expressed as G = {0, 1, 2,..., 255}. As a rule; 0 gray level corresponds to black color, 255 gray level refers to white color, and gray levels between these values correspond to gray tones. The figure shows 256 different gray levels on a grid of N × M = 16 × 16.

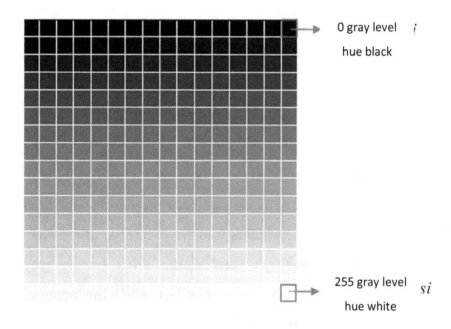

0 gray level ¡
hue black

255 gray level si
hue white

Color Image:

Color images are formed by displaying three gray-level images of the same object encoded in R (Red), G (Green), B (Blue) in a row. These three colors, the color of which forms the image, are called bands.

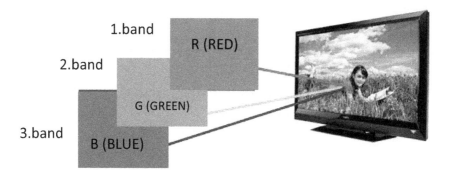

Each pixel of the color images is displayed on computer screens as 24-bit data. Namely, since each color will be encoded with 8 bits (2.2.2.2.2.2.2.2 = 2^8 = 256), three colors (RGB) will be encoded with 3x8 = 24 bits. In this case, each pixel of RGB images can have $2^8.2^8.2^8 = 2^{24}$ = 16.777.216 (about 17 million) different color values, and the value range of the combination of these three colors is RGB = (0, 0, 0),..., (255 , 255, 255) format. Some sample colors and values are given in the table below.

Color	HTML / CSS Name	Hex Code #RRGGBB	Decimal Code (R,G,B)
	Black	#000000	(0,0,0)
	White	#FFFFFF	(255,255,255)
	Red	#FF0000	(255,0,0)
	Lime	#00FF00	(0,255,0)
	Blue	#0000FF	(0,0,255)
	Yellow	#FFFF00	(255,255,0)
	Cyan / Aqua	#00FFFF	(0,255,255)
	Magenta / Fuchsia	#FF00FF	(255,0,255)
	Silver	#C0C0C0	(192,192,192)
	Gray	#808080	(128,128,128)
	Maroon	#800000	(128,0,0)

Color	HTML / CSS Name	Hex Code #RRGGBB	Decimal Code (R,G,B)
	Olive	#808000	(128,128,0)
	Green	#008000	(0,128,0)
	Purple	#800080	(128,0,128)
	Teal	#008080	(0,128,128)
	Navy	#000080	(0,0,128)

Considering the meaning of the matrix, a naturally colored 2D RGB image consists of three matrices (grids) each (N × M) in size, and the {I (i, j, k) | i = 1, 2,..., N; j = 1, 2,..., M; It is represented in the form k = 1, 2, 3}. In general, each of these matrices represents an image whose pixels have one of 256 levels.

I (i, j, 1); i = 1, 2,..., N, j = 1, 2,..., M → Matrix for the red band
I (i, j, 2); i = 1, 2,..., N, j = 1, 2,..., M → Matrix for green tape
I (i, j, 3); i = 1, 2,..., N, j = 1, 2,..., M → Matrix for the blue band

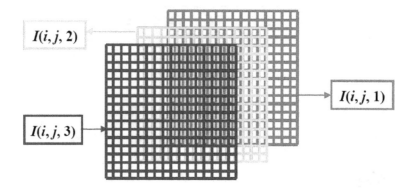

Figure 3.4. Matrix representation of 3 bands in NxM dimensions that make up the RGB image.

By taking zero images of the green and blue bands of the color image, only the red band image is obtained. Thus, the RGB representation reaches the red artificially colored image. In this case, the encoding will be RGB = R00 = (0, 0, 0),..., (255, 0, 0). Similarly, green and blue artificially colored images are also RGB = 0G0 = ((Natural color imagery (RGB) = 00B = (0, 0, 0),..., (0, 0, 255). Artificial coloring images formed in this way will be as follows.

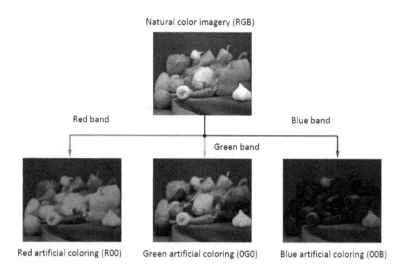

Natural color imagery (RGB)

Red band

Blue band

Green band

Red artificial coloring (R00)   Green artificial coloring (0G0)   Blue artificial coloring (00B)

For a color image consisting of natural colors in RGB format, the correct combination of bands should be 1-2-3 (Red, Green, Blue) respectively. In the figure below, the gray-tone image of the natural color, in which the three colors come together, and the individual gray-tone image of each band are given.

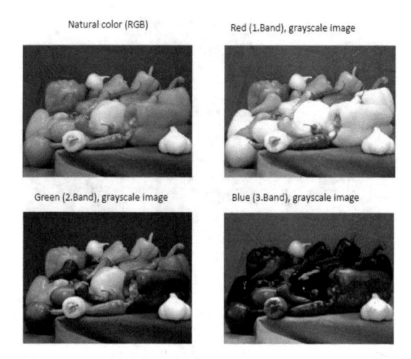

Natural color (RGB) · Red (1.Band), grayscale image

Green (2.Band), grayscale image · Blue (3.Band), grayscale image

Figure 3.5. A natural color image and grayscale images of this image's RGB tapes.

If the band joints are changed in RGB notation, the colors will also change. Images formed in this way are called artificial color images. The pictures below show examples of this.

Natural color, band mixing (1-2-3)

artificial color image, band mixing (2-1-3)

artificial color image, band mixing (1-3-2)

artificial color image, band mixing (2-3-1)

Figure 3.6. A natural color RGB image and artificial color images derived from this image.

Converting the color image to Gray-Tone

The process of converting a color numeric image into a gray-toned image is actually nothing more than scaling gray-toned images that correspond to each color band specified in the RGB color model. In this sense, the scaling process performed by sticking to the brightness values of the color image is given by the formula given above using the formula *gray = 0.299 x R + 0.587 x G + 0.114 x B*. By using this equation, the gray image of the color image is obtained.

Natural color (RGB)

Figure 3.7. Obtaining a grayscale image from a natural color image.

Memory Space Covered by Digital Image

The number of bits required to store a numerical image of size (N × M), each pixel represented by m bits, consisting of N rows and M columns, is calculated as follows: b = NMm, (bits)

It is calculated as 8 bit = 1byte, 1024 byte = 1Kbyte, 1024 Kbyte = 1Mbyte. Accordingly, it can be calculated how much space an image with a pixel ranging from 1 to 8 bits will occupy.

For example, if a gray image represented by 8 bits per pixel is NxM = 1000x600 pixels

b = 1000x600x8 = 4.800.000 bits / 8 = 600.000 bytes = 600 Kbytes = 0.6 Mbytes.

73

If we store the same image with a 24-bit encoding (color image) (each pixel is shown in RGB = $2^8 + 2^8 + 2^8 = 2^{24}$ = 16.777.216 million colors)

b = 1000x600x24 = 14.400.000 bits / 8 = 1.800.000 bytes = 1.800 Kbytes = 1.8 Mbytes.

As the number of bits required to encode each pixel increases, the amount of memory required to store the image increases. As a result, color images take up more space in computers in terms of memory than gray-tone images. For example; An 8-bit image is 3Mbyte, while for a gray-toned image this value is 1Mbyte.

Resolution - (Field Sensitivity and Color Brightness Sensitivity)

The resolution of an image is the degree of detail in the image. This concept contains both Field resolution and Brightness resolution. The area resolution indicates the number of samples taken from the surface (N x M) and the Brightness resolution indicates the brightness (m) of the color on the pixel as the gray level equivalent. The greater the increase in the values of these parameters, the more the digitized image approaches the original. However, the memory space occupied by the image increases rapidly.

Field Accuracy (Pixel resolution)

Area sensitivity is related to the number of samples collected during horizontal / vertical scanning of the analog image in order to obtain the digital image. The greater the number of pixels (N × M) that make up the digital image, the closer the original (analog) image is. On the other hand, if the number of pixels is reduced, then the spatial resolution of the image decreases and the details in the image begin to disappear. This is called the checkerboard effect. This effect results in the formation of artificial frames within the image. The following figure shows 8-bit grayscale images with various field resolutions. As can be seen, as the number of pixels decreases, the checkerboard effect increases.

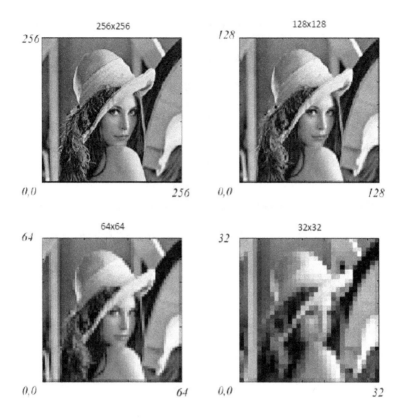

Figure 3.8. Sample images with different area resolutions, each pixel represented by 8 bits.

3.2.16 Brightness sensitivity (gray-level color resolution)

The brightness sensitivity shows the number of gray pixels on the gray level scale, which corresponds to the brightness of each pixel. In other words, 256 steps (8 bits) were used in the gray level scale, while turning the color from black to white. Instead of the gray color on this scale, the equivalent of any color will show the brightness of that color.

As stated earlier, the gray-tone images commonly used in the application have a full brightness value of 255 in terms of gray level, which corresponds to the white color. That is, the pixels of such images can have 256 different values, including the gray level range of G = {0, 1, 2,..., 255}, and as a result, each pixel is represented by m = 8 bits. As the number of gray levels decreases, artificial line lines begin to appear in the image. 256 colors (8 bits), 128 colors (7 bits), 64 colors (6 bits), 32 colors (5 bits), 16 colors (4 bits), 8 colors (3 bits), 4 colors (2 bits) as below and gray-tone images with the same field resolution (NxM = 256x256), which is 2 colors (1 bit).

When the images are examined, the differences between 8 bits and 5 bits are not fully understood with the naked eye (a bit more color would emerge though). However, it can be clearly seen that the quality drops between 4 bits and 1 bits, and artificial borders are noticed.

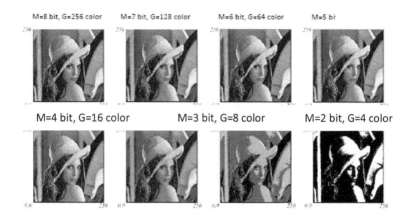

Figure 3.9. Displays in-kind resolution gray-tones with various gray-level color resolutions.

3.3 image softening (blurring) blurring filters

In image processing, digital filters are used to soften the image or make the edges clear. In this section, picture smoothing will be discussed. For this purpose, the following filters will be examined.

- Average Filter (Mean)
- Medium Value Filter (Median)
Gaussian Smoothing
- Conservative Soomthing
- Crimmins Speckle Removal
- Frequency Filters

In filtering, the input image is converted with h (i, j) with the f (i, j) filter function to process. This expression can be shown mathematically as follows. $g(i,j) = h(i,j) \odot f(i,j)$

78

Convolution process; A core template (matrix / kernel) can be defined as the 'scroll and multiply' operation of pixels on the image. In this process, the core template is shifted on the image and its value is multiplied by the appropriate pixels on the image.

There are several standard templates for certain special applications. Here, the size and shape of the template determine the properties of the process. For example, the mean and templates of the Laplace operator (core matrices) are as follows.

1/9	1/9	1/9
1/9	1/9	1/9
1/9	1/9	1/9

Mean

0	-1	0
-1	4	-1
0	-1	0

Laplacian

Average filter (mean filter -box blur)

Common names; Mean filtering, Smoothing, Averaging, Box filtering.

Average filter is a simple and easy-to-apply method of smoothing images. In other words, it is to reduce the amount of change between one pixel and others. It is often used to reduce noise in images.

Average filter is to replace each pixel value of an image with the average value of its neighbors and itself. This leads to the disappearance of pixel values that do not represent the surroundings. The average filter is a convolution filter. Convolution filters are based on the core template (kernel). As shown in the figure, mostly 3 × 3 square core template is used. In some smoothing operations larger templates (such as 5 × 5, 7x7) can be used. An effect similar to the effect of the large template on a single scan can also be achieved with multiple passes of the small template.

1/9	1/9	1/9
1/9	1/9	1/9
1/9	1/9	1/9

Mean

Figure 3.10. 3 × 3 average template, often used in the average filter.

The average filter is the simplest method to reduce noise in an image. However, while the noise is made less pronounced, the image is softened. If the size of the core template (matrix) used is increased, softening will increase even more.

There are two main problems with average filtering:

a) A pixel with a value that does not represent the picture very well affects the average value of all the pixels in the near region. This causes the picture to change.

b) As the filter (template) passes over an edge, it will generate new values for the pixels on both sides of the edge, which will cause the edge to become blurred. This may be an issue if sharp edges are not lost.

To solve these two problems, Median Filter was developed instead of Mean filter. However, this filter also takes a long time to calculate. One of the commonly used filters for official softening is the "Gaussian smoothing filter".

Normal picture

3x3 template

5x5 template

7x7 template

3.3.1 median filter

Common names of this filter are; Median filter (Median filtering), Rank filtering The median filter is normally used to reduce noise in an image, such as mean filter. However, it does much better than the mean filter at the point that the details on the picture are not lost. Like the mean filter, the median filter looks at its neighbors nearby to calculate the value of each pixel. Instead of replacing the pixel value with the average of the neighboring pixel values in the median filter (mean filter), it sorts the neighboring pixels and takes the value in the middle of the row. If the examined area (inside the template) has an even number of pixels, the average of the two pixels in the middle is used as the middle value.

If we do our operations according to the middle pixel in the figure below, we can see that the value of this pixel does not represent the pixels around 150, well. When changing the value of this pixel, let's first line up the value of the surrounding pixels. These consist of values (115, 119, 120, 123, 124, 125, 126, 127,150). In the middle of these values, there are 124 numbers. Accordingly, the number 150 is replaced by the number 124. Here the number 124 becomes the median number (middle value). The template used here is 3x3 pixels in size. Using larger templates produces more smoothing (smoothing) effects.

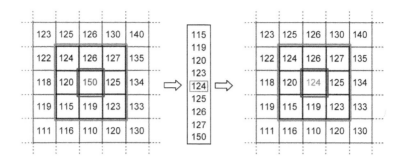

The median filter has two advantages over the Mean filter.

- Using the median represents the template more strongly than using the mean. Since the ability to represent will remain at the ends of the array lined up in a distant pixel (it will never be present), it becomes impossible for it to affect the overall representation of the neighbors there.

- The median value (middle value) does not generate unrealistic pixel values when moving along the edge, as neighboring pixels should be the value. For this reason, the median filter protects the sharp edges better than the mean filter. If it exemplifies, the middle value is either black or white at a border of black and white. The average of the two will not be gray. Thus, the sharpness on the edge will not be lost.

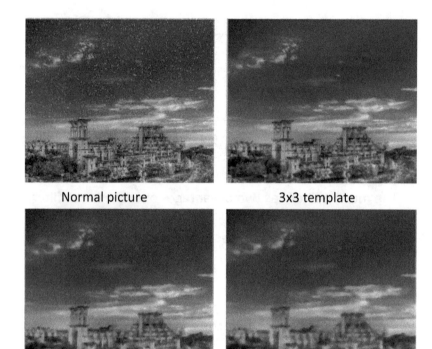

| Normal picture | 3x3 template |
| 5x5 template | 7x7 template |

3.3.2 gaussian smoothing

The Gaussian softening operator is a 2-dimensional convolution (multiplication of the core matrix and the pixels on the image) operator used to 'blur' images and eliminate detail and noise. In this sense, it is similar to the Mean filter. However, Gauss uses a different core template (matrix) that can be represented by the "bell-shaped" graphic pictured below. If the formula that gives the bell-shaped graph of Gauss is written for the 2D plane and 3D space, it can be shown in the figure below.

$$G(x) = \frac{1}{\sqrt{2\pi}\,\sigma} e^{-\frac{x^2}{2\sigma}}$$

$$G(x) = \frac{1}{\sqrt{2\pi}\,\sigma^2} e^{-\frac{x^2+y^2}{2\sigma^2}}$$

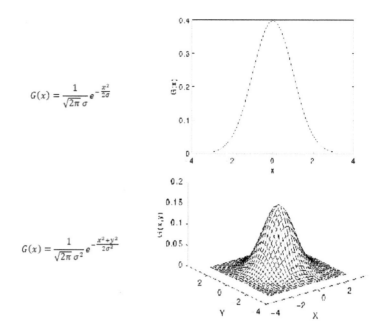

Here σ is the standard deviation of the distribution. Also, the mean of the distribution is assumed to be zero (i.e. centered on the line x = 0). The 2D and 3D graphics have axially symmetrical values. If we draw the two-dimensional chart in Excel in the range of x = ∓2 for Standard deviation σ = 1, we get the following chart.

3.4 Sharpening Filter

This algorithm reveals the image of prominent edges by removing the image softened from the original image. Later, it combines the image of the original image with the edges that have become prominent, resulting in a sharpened

86

image (sharpened image). Image sharpening is widely used in the photogrammetry and printing industry.

G (x, y) output image, f (x, y) input image, and fsmooth (x, y) in softened version of this image can be shown as follows.

$$g(x,y) = f(x,y) - f_{smooth}(x,y) \rightarrow f_{smooth}(x,y) = f(x,y) - k^* g(x,y)$$

Here k is a scaling constant. Reasonable values for k range from 0.2-0.7. As k grows, the amount of sharpening increases.

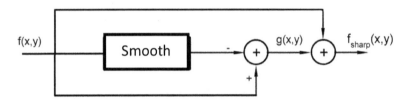

We can better understand the process by examining the frequency response of the filter. If we have a signal like the one below (a) lowpass filtering (edges are softened) from this signal (b) highpass image (sharp edges) appears (c). If these sharp edges are combined with the original image, a sharpened (sharpened edges) image is created (d).

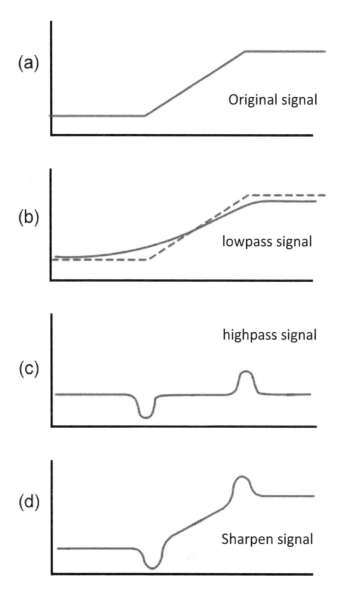

Figure 3.11. Calculating edge image with frequency response for the sharpen filter.

Sharpen filter is done by convolution process. In other words, by using a core matrix, it is moved over the image area and new image is obtained with necessary multiplication operations. The mean filter of 3x3 can be used to create a softened version of the image. The softened image is then subtracted from the original image over pixel values. The values occurring at this time may be negative or exceed 255. In this case, it is necessary to normalize the values.

Normalizing the values: If the R, G, B values in the image are out of the 0-255 values at the end of the mathematical operations, it is necessary to normalize the values by subjecting the whole picture to the same proportion.

If we show the limit values in the picture with a, b, 0,255 numbers, which are the interval that these values should be, with c, d, and the value to be normalized with Pin, Pout in the normalized state, we can formulate this process as follows. Note that this formula is a stretching process by establishing the ratio in the given ranges.

$$\frac{(b-a)}{(d-c)} = \frac{(P_{in}-a)}{(P_{out}-c)} \rightarrow \boxed{P_{out} = (P_{in}-a)\left(\frac{d-c}{b-a}\right) + c}$$

Examples;

$$P_{out} = (120 - (-30)) \left(\frac{255 - 0}{330 - (-30)} \right) + 0 = 106$$

Note: If the upper and lower limits here do not exceed 0 and 255, d and c numbers cannot be taken as 0 and 255. The more internal values (b or a) should be taken. Otherwise, there are no white or black areas, and these regions begin to emerge.

Original Picture   Blurring with Mean 9x9 matrix

Edge Image   Image sharpened by mean 9x9 matrix

Sharpened image with Gauss (5x5) matrix

If the original picture is blurry at the beginning, the size of the matrix used should be increased. Since the Gauss process blurs more precisely, the effect will look better on fine images.

This chapter cannot be shortened because the complexity and multitude of topics and languages in it, so I recommend reading my book **"Step by step web design with visual studio 2019[1]"** on web design by academy way easy and simple and fast , here I will explain a simple website design in Visual Studio.

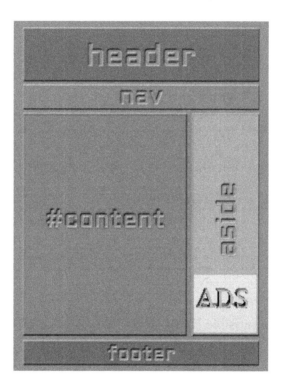

---

[1] You can see the book on my blog "https://dr-eng-mohammed-ridha.blogspot.com/"

4.1 Basic concepts

www: **World Wide Web** is the abbreviated form of the word. The alternate name is W3. It is a system created to connect sites to the Internet. The word "Web" in the term "new search engines on the Web" is dedicated to the WWW.

W3C: **World Wide Web Consortium** is the abbreviation of the words. It is an international community that sets and develops Web standards.

HTML: **HyperText Markup Language** is the abbreviation of the words. The main markup language used to display web pages.

XML: Description **eXtensible Markup Language** It shaped. It is a markup language developed for coding files for both people and machines to read. Unlike HTML, XML tags can be defined specifically by the user. It is often used to create sitemaps on websites.

XHTML: **eXtensible HTML** is the abbreviation of the words. XML and HTML is a composite state. It was developed by W3C to minimize errors caused by the highly flexible structure in HTML.

Domain: The alternative name is "domain name". Web site is the name on the internet. For example;

denemex1denemex2.com is a domain. It has an IP address on its basis. Such a system has been developed because it is difficult for users to type this IP address and access sites.

Hosting: In order for domain names to be accessed 24/7, the service provided by various companies is called hosting. Hosting companies have servers that work in the morning without closing, in other words, they have servers. The website owner sends the site documents to these servers and enables the site to be visited by the whole world.

SSL/TLS: **Transport Layer Security** is predecessor / predecessor, Secure Sockets Layer, is a protocol designed to provide secure communication over a computer network.

HTTP: **HyperText Transfer Protocol** is the abbreviation of the words. Site names are written in http: // before www. As the name implies, this protocol is based on W3C to display the sites on our screen. It has been developed to put certain standards of data transfer between a website and a server. A more secure version of this transfer, HTTPS (HTTP Secure) is used today to ensure data security on all commercial shopping sites.

FTP: It is **File Transfer Protocol**. It is a protocol created by the website owner to send the site files to the server. FTP software has been developed to allow website owners to access servers. Although SmartFTP has many software such as CuteFTP, it is the most popular FileZilla software. It is very simple to use.

HTTP, Determining the relationship between **(visitor ~ server)**; FTP, determines the relationship between **(client ~ server)**.

SEO: **Search Engine Optimization** is the abbreviation of the words. In order for sites to be indexed by search engines, HTML tags are written in some definitions. The subject of SEO is a field of study in its own right and we will discuss this in the future.

HTML Etiketi: < > the square brackets you see in the form is written. For example; <title> is a label. </ title> indicates that the label is closed.

4.2   Web Programming Languages

Before entering the explanation, you must know that strabismus in the world of web design must know the language of HTML and the CSS of these two languages are sufficient to design a rigid site or in other words static, it means to add something new that is compelled to add it from the code and upload it to the site.

But in order to design a dynamic website, you must know the JavaScript language and one of the Back-end languages such as PHP or Asp.net with SQL.

Important note that you should not forget your site must be responsive, that is, it is responsive to different screen sizes.

HTML5: Is a web standard developed in the 80s by Tim Berners-Lee, who works as a contractor in CERN, which is short of the words hyper text markup language: HTML is a web standard that was developed in the 80s by Tim Berners-Lee, who works in

CERN. Tim Berners-Lee is also the founder of the W3C, whose opening WorldWideWeb Consortium. This part is important to you because the W3C is an international organization that sets the standard for all web browsers today.

CSS3: Is **C**ascading **S**tyle **S**heets. It is used to make the code written in HTML more visually rich. For example; You can change the text colors of paragraphs from a single point with CSS. This place is important; because before CSS was released, we had to define individual styles for each HTML tag. Along with CSS, this problem has disappeared. Now with a single file, we can shape the content on all our pages.

JavaScript : A web page consists of three basic elements: **content**, **presentation** and **interaction**. The content portion represents HTML, the presentation portion is CSS, and the interaction part represents JavaScript. If we have a project consisting only of content and presentation, we can describe this website as a **static** website. If we use interactivity with these two elements, we will create a dynamic website. **Dynamic** sites are interactive and visitors can perform some activities with the commands they give on the web page. For example; the user has filled out the contact form; but he forgot to write his email address. Then press "Send" button. After you press the button, a warning window pops up and "you forgot to write your e-mail

97

address!" in the form of a warning. Here is the technology that allows this warning window to be generated.

 **jQuery** : Is a JavaScript library. Until 2006, too much complex JavaScript library was used. John Resig developed jQuery to make these JavaScript libraries simpler and more understandable. Then it offered it to the web developers. In a few years, jQuery became popular all over the world.

 **SQL**: "**S**tructured **Q**uery **L**anguage" is a non-procedural programming language, and thus differs from the usual programming languages such as C or Java, as non-procedural languages are specialized languages. Therefore, the syntax of the Structured Query Language is a language for dealing and controlling the interconnected databases by dealing with data structures, performing data entry operations, deletions, sorting, searching, filtering, modifying, etc.

 **MySQL** is a relational database management system that works with SQL. Hc was given this name according to the daughter of his original programmer, Michael Widenius, who was named MySQL. MySQL is a

component of the LAMP web application software stack (and others), which is an acronym for Linux, Apache, MySQL, Perl / PHP / Python. MySQL is used by many database-driven web applications, including Drupal, Joomla, phpBB, and WordPress. MySQL is also used by many popular websites.

 **PHP**: Hypertext Preprocessor. It is a scripting language primarily designed to be used for developing and programming web applications. It can also be used to produce standalone programs that are not related to the web only. PHP is an open source language and developed by a team of volunteers under the license of PHP, it supports object-oriented programming and its structural structure is very similar to the structural installation of the C language, in addition to that it works on multiple operating systems such as Linux and Windows.

 **ASP.NET:** "Active Server Pages" which means is a framework for web applications developed and marketed by Microsoft Corporation, in order to give programmers the ability to build dynamic websites, web applications and web services. It was released in January 2002 with version 1.0 of the dot net

framework, and this technology is a successor to the ASP technology (active server pages). Also, ASP.NET was built to build on CLR (inter-language runtime) technology, which allows programmers to write their own code for the ASP.NET framework using whatever programming language they prefer to be supported by the .net framework.

4.3   Create the Basic WebSite

Now we're running visual studio community 2019 first before we start creating the project.

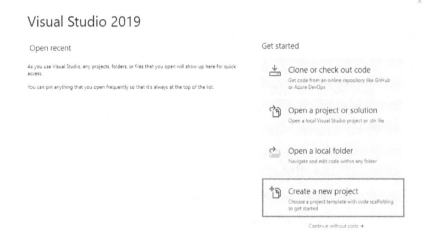

Figure 4.1. Creating a new project.

We click on **Create new project** and we're starting to create our new project.

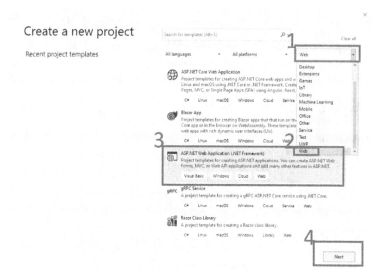

Figure 4.2. Select ASP.NET web Application (.Net framework).

Then, we select **web** from **project type**, then select **"ASP.NET Web Application (.Net Framework)"**, then press Next,

After clicking on the next, a page comes to us, specifying the name and location of the project, and don't forget to specify the last version of .NET Framework 4.7.2, and in the location, choose where you want to save it as your omputer, defulat saving in the "C:\Users\yourComputerName\source\repos". And click Create if everything is OK.

101

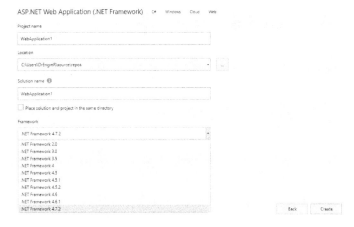

Configure your new project

ASP.NET Web Application (.NET Framework)   C#   Windows   Cloud   Web

Project name

WebApplication1

Location

C:\Users\DrEnginR\source\repos

Solution name

WebApplication1

☐ Place solution and project in the same directory

Framework

.NET Framework 4.7.2

.NET Framework 2.0
.NET Framework 3.0
.NET Framework 3.5
.NET Framework 4
.NET Framework 4.5
.NET Framework 4.5.1
.NET Framework 4.5.2
.NET Framework 4.6
.NET Framework 4.6.1
.NET Framework 4.7.2

Back   Create

Figure 4.3. configure your new project.

Select Empty from Templates. And select MVC then click Create.

Create a new ASP.NET Web Application

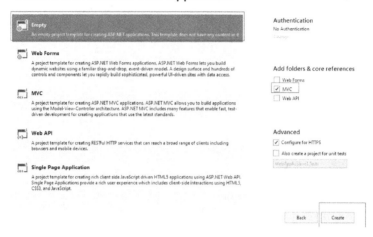

Empty
An empty project template for creating ASP.NET applications. This template does not have any content in it

Web Forms
A project template for creating ASP.NET Web Forms applications. ASP.NET Web Forms lets you build dynamic websites using a familiar drag-and-drop, event-driven model. A design surface and hundreds of controls and components let you rapidly build sophisticated, powerful UI-driven sites with data access.

MVC
A project template for creating ASP.NET MVC applications. ASP.NET MVC allows you to build applications using the Model-View-Controller architecture. ASP.NET MVC includes many features that enable fast, test-driven development for creating applications that use the latest standards.

Web API
A project template for creating RESTful HTTP services that can reach a broad range of clients including browsers and mobile devices.

Single Page Application
A project template for creating rich client side JavaScript driven HTML5 applications using ASP.NET Web API. Single Page Applications provide a rich user experience which includes client-side interactions using HTML5, CSS3, and JavaScript.

Authentication
No Authentication

Add folders & core references
- Web Forms
- ☑ MVC
- Web API

Advanced
- ☑ Configure for HTTPS
- Also create a project for unit tests

Back   Create

Figure 4.4.Create a new ASP.NET Web Application.

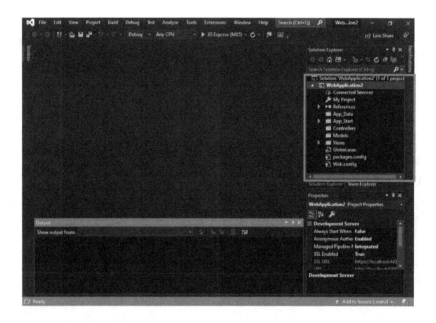

Figure 4.5. Solution window.

103

Depending on the speed of your processor, your project will be created after a while and you will see an image in this way. You can see the project contents from the **Solution Explorer** window.

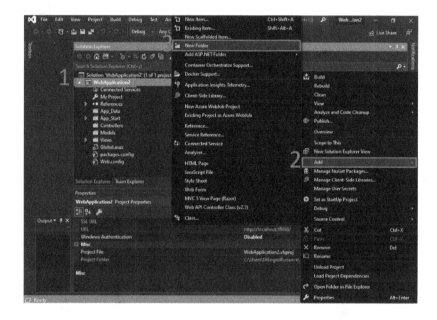

Figure 4.6. Adding new folder.

In Solution Explorer, right-click the WebApplication2[2] post, and then click Add> New Folder.

---

[2] This is your project name, don't worry about that

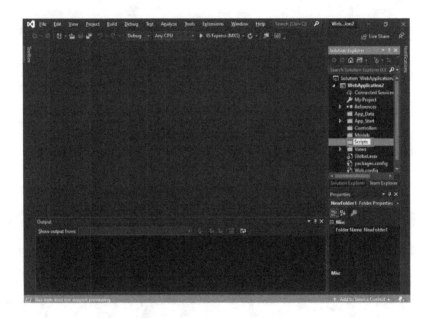

Figure 4.7. Give name for folder.

Name the folder as Scripts,

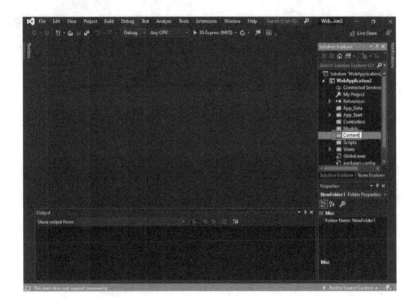

Figure 4.8. Create another folder and give name.

Create a folder in the same way and give it the name as Content.

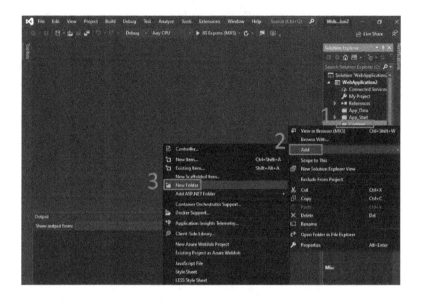

Figure 4.9. Create a new folder in the Content folder.

Right-click the Content folder and follow **Add> New Folder**.

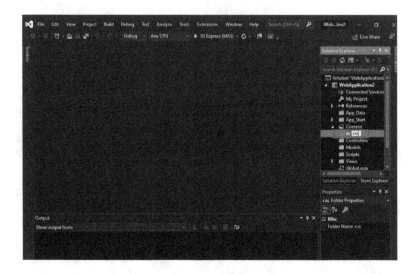

Figure 4.10. css creates a folder in the Content folder.

Create a new folder and give it **css** name.

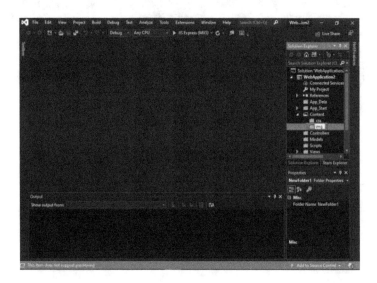

Figure 4.11. img creates a folder in the Content folder.

In the same way, add another folder named **img** into the
Content folder.

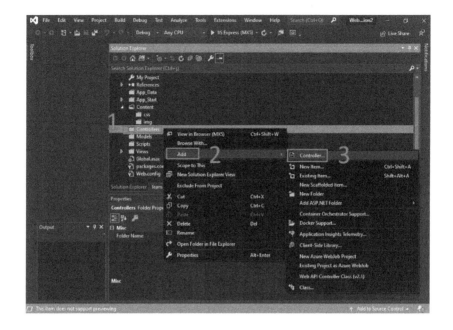

Figure 4.12. Adding Controller.

Now we start the MVC 5 event. **Right-click** the **Controllers** folder and follow **Add> Controller**.

108

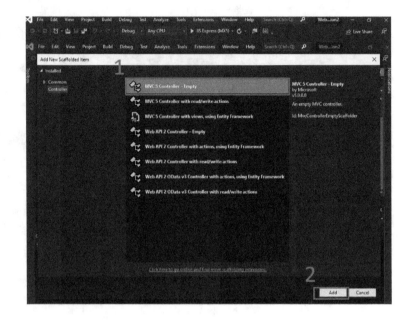

Figure 4.13. Adding Controller.

Select **MVC5 Controller-Empty**, then click add.

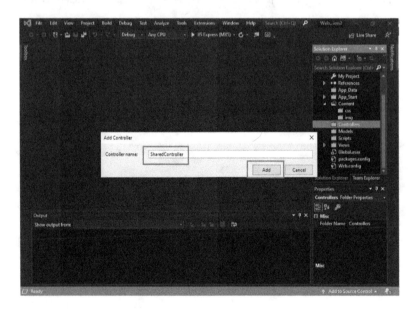

Figure 4.14. Creating SharedController.vb.

Delete the **Default** name of the controller and type **SharedController**. Then click **Add**.

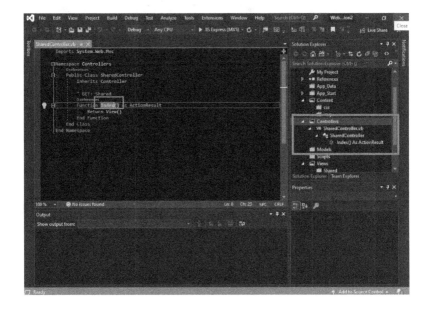

Figure 4.15. rename index to _Layout.

110

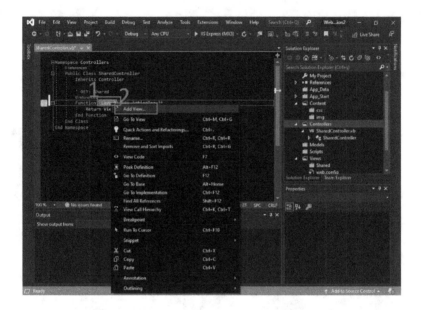

Figure 4.16. Add View.

You will see a source code called SharedController.cs has been added into the Controllers folder. On this page, delete the part that says **Index** and type **_Layout** instead. Then **right-click _Layout** and follow **Add View**.

Deselect Use a layout or master page. This page will be our layout already. Then click Add.

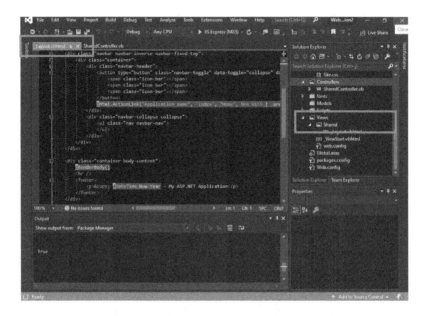

You will see a folder named Shared in the **Views** folder and a file named **_Layout.vbhtml**. This is our layout page. The content is as you see in the image.

I'm doing a few minor edits on this page. First, I delete the field above the **<! DOCTYPE html>** document type **declaration**. I'm adding two new **meta** tags with my site description and the **keywords**. These two labels are the basic commodities for **SEO** (search engine optimization). I'm writing **@ViewBag.Title** into my **<title>** tag. In this way, the titles of other pages will be read from layout. Then I delete the **<body>** tag and write **@RenderBody ()**. So the contents of my other pages can be read with @RenderBody ().

Right-click the **Controllers folder** again and follow **Add> Controller**.

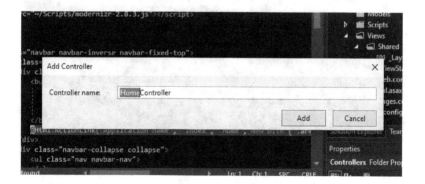

Change the controller name to **HomeController** and click **Add**. This controller will be the content of our homepage.

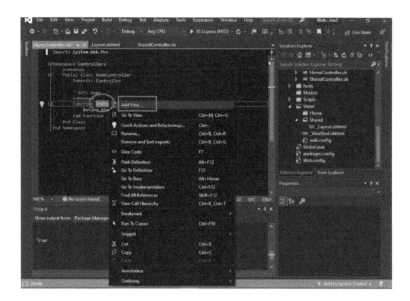

You will see a source code called **HomeController.vb** in the Controllers folder. Do not change the **Index** section of this page; then right click on Index. Follow **Add View**.

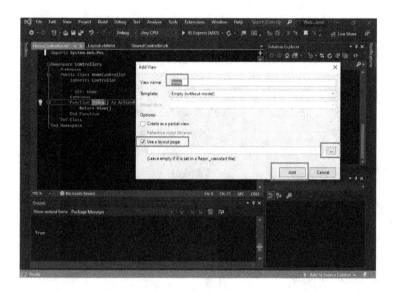

Check the **Use a layout** or **masterpage** box this time and click the button named.

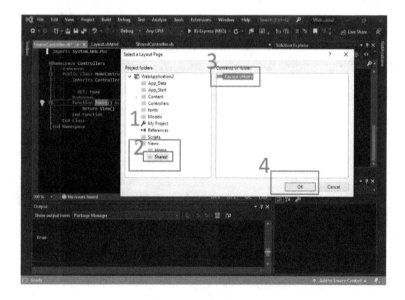

Select _Layout.vbhtml from there and click OK.

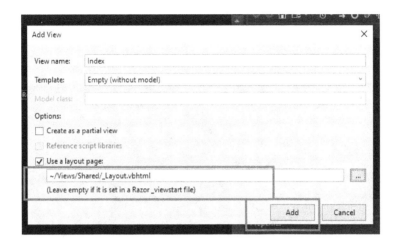

Here is the main page of the content of the main page to be read from the layout page. In this way, specify the file path, and then click Add.

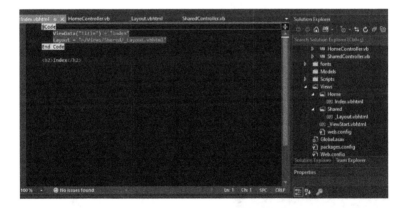

You will see a folder called Home in the Views folder and a file called Index.vbhtml. This will be the page with the

116

contents of our homepage. The content should be as you see

on the image.

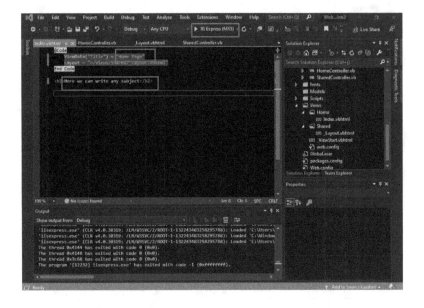

Figure 4.17. Run.

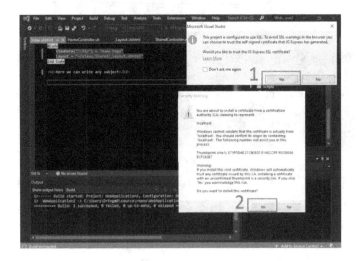

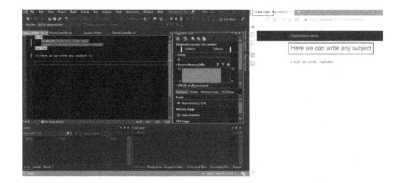

We'll make a few minor edits on this page. First I replaced page title "index" to "Home page" and replaced "<h2>index</h2>" to "<h2>Here we can write any subject</h2>" Then I click on the IIS Express (MX5)[3] we're running our project for the first time and we'll test it for the first time.

As we have seen, our project works successfully. Our page title is "Home Page" and our content is " Here we can write any subject" shaped

---

[3] Don't worry, I using a Maxthon browser web, and the MX5 is shortcut, You will have the shortcut displayed to your default browser, so there is no problem.

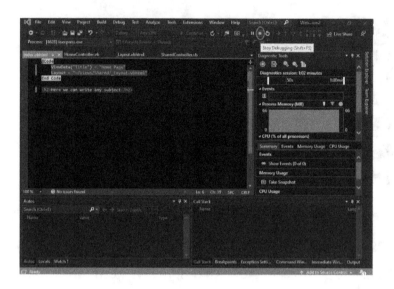

Press the red stop button to stop the project.

4.3.1 Creating the Menu

Now we will create our menu. First I delete the background color of my nav and #content elements.

1 /* *** nav *** */

2   nav {

3   width: 960px;

4   height: 40px;

5   line-height: 40px;

6   text-align: center;

```
7        position: relative;

8    }

9    .nav-item {

10       width: 191px;

11       height: 38px;

12       position: relative;

13       float: left;

14       border: 1px solid black;

15       border-left: 0;

16       background: royalblue;

17       color: white;

18       font-size: 16px;

19    }
```

I'm setting a class named .nav-item under my nav picker. This class will have links to our menu.

float: left with the menu elements left in the nav I'll lean.

The edge thickness except the left will be 1px black. The background color is blue.

Text color will be white and 16px.

```
1    <nav>

2    <div class="nav-item">

3    <span>Home</span>

4    </div>

5    <div class="nav-item">

6    <span>About Us</span>

7    </div>

8    <div class="nav-item">

9    <span>References</span>

10   </div>

11   <div class="nav-item">

12   <span>Solutions</span>

13   </div>
```

```
14   <div class="nav-item" style="width: 192px; border-
     right: 0">

15   <span>Contact</span>

16   </div>

17   </nav>
```

In the nav tag, I'm adding the .nav-item classes and typing the menu names in the <span> tag.

I simply raise the right border of the last menu item and increase its width by 1px. I could do this from CSS; but the goal is to see the change more easily. Now I'm working on my project.

Our menu's okay. This way you must have an image. We'll give the menu links the next time we create subpages.

4.3.2   Creating the Content

Now let's fill in our #content div. Delete the height value of # content. It will automatically be

```
1          /* *** content *** */

2          #content {

3             width: 920px;

4             padding: 20px;

5             position: relative;

6             text-align: justify;

7          }

8          #content h1 {

9             font-size: 18px;

10            text-align: center;

11         }

12         .img-left {

13            width: 260px;

14            float: left;
```

```
15          margin: 0 10px 10px 0;

16     }
```

In this way, our #content selector features. I erased the height. I gave her a 20px gap. For this reason, I set the width to 920px instead of 960px like other components. This is due to the fact that 20px gives the right and 20px to the left.

(960px - 20px right - 20px left = 920px)

The properties of the title in the content of the properties of h1 code, such as whether.

I define a class named .img-left to justify the image that we will use in the content. float: left with a left visual. margin: 0 10px 10px 0 with the right and down to give a 10-pixel pixel space. Thus, the picture and content will not appear in the bottom.

```
1      <section id="content">

2         @RenderBody()

3      </section>
```

If you remember, we have defined @RenderBody () in our #content element. Therefore, we should add the contents of this element on the main page instead of filling it in layout.

Open the Views> home> Index.vbhtml page. So our homepage.

```
1   @{

2       ViewBag.Title = "Home page";

3       Layout = "~/Shared/_Layout.vbhtml";

4   }

5

6   <h1>Ana Sayfa</h1>

7   <img src="~/Content/img/1.png" alt="Image title"
    class="img-left" />

8   <p>

9       What is Lorem Ipsum?

10  </p>

11  <p>
```

12   <b>Lorem Ipsum</b> is simply dummy text of the printing and typesetting industry. Lorem Ipsum has been the industry's standard dummy text ever since the 1500s, when an unknown printer took a galley of type and scrambled it to make a type specimen book. It has survived not only five centuries, but also the leap into electronic typesetting, remaining essentially unchanged. It was popularised in the 1960s with the release of Letraset sheets containing Lorem Ipsum passages, and more recently with desktop publishing software like Aldus PageMaker including versions of Lorem Ipsum.

13   </p>

14   <p>

15   Where does it come from?

16   </p>

17   <p>

18   Contrary to popular belief, Lorem Ipsum is not simply random text. It has roots in a piece of classical Latin literature from 45 BC, making it over 2000 years old. Richard McClintock, a Latin professor at

Hampden-Sydney College in Virginia, looked up one of the more obscure Latin words, consectetur, from a Lorem Ipsum passage, and going through the cites of the word in classical literature, discovered the undoubtable source. Lorem Ipsum comes from sections 1.10.32 and 1.10.33 of "de Finibus Bonorum et Malorum" (The Extremes of Good and Evil) by Cicero, written in 45 BC. This book is a treatise on the theory of ethics, very popular during the Renaissance. The first line of Lorem Ipsum, "Lorem ipsum dolor sit amet..", comes from a line in section 1.10.32.

19   </p>

20   <p>

21   The standard chunk of Lorem Ipsum used since the 1500s is reproduced below for those interested. Sections 1.10.32 and 1.10.33 from "de Finibus Bonorum et Malorum" by Cicero are also reproduced in their exact original form, accompanied by English versions from the 1914 translation by H. Rackham.

22   </p>

Go to **lipsum.org** and add text to content. Add the image.jpg file between the title and the grammar and set the class to img-left.

You should have obtained such an image when you run the project.

4.3.3   Creating the footer

Finally, we will complete the footer area, which contains the details of our site.

```
1    /* *** footer *** */
```

```
2        footer {

3            width: 960px;

4            height: 60px;

5            line-height: 60px;

6            text-align: center;

7            position: relative;

8            border-top: 1px solid black;

9            color: white;

10           background: royalblue;

11       }
```

I'm making a little change here. I set the background color to blue and the text color to white.

```
1    <footer>

2    <p>&copy; @DateTime.Now.Year - All Rights
     Reserved | Designed by Dr. Eng. Mohammed Ridha
     Faisal</p>

3    </footer>
```

I wrote the site information in the <small> tag to the content on my layout page.

When I run my project, I'll get a screenshot like this. This is how I complete my home page.

You have completed the third step. In the next section, we'll touch on adding sub-pages and completing the project.

Programming mobile applications is no less size and complex than programming web sites, and we cannot shorten it significantly, and as you know our book gives an overview and a simple but beneficial for students of computer engineering, so I will suffice to explain the programming of mobile applications on a simple example and it is Calculator design.

5.1   Mobile Operating Systems

Android: is a free and open source operating system based on the Linux kernel, designed primarily for touch screen devices such as smartphones and tablets. The Android system has been developed by the Open Alliance for Mobile Phones managed by Google. The Android system user interface is mainly based on direct processing, using touch gestures that are largely compatible with realistic movements, such as clicking, scanning, and fingerprinting, in order to manipulate objects on the screen panel, as well as the default keyboard for entering text. Google has developed touch devices as well as Android TV sets for TVs, Android Auto cars, and Android Wear watches. As each developed with a special user interface. Types of

131

Android systems are also used on laptop computers, game consoles, digital cameras, and other electronic devices.

iOS: (known at its beginnings as iPhone OSX, OSX iPhone and its previous official name until June 7, 2010 is: iPhone OS or iPhone OS) is an operating system that appeared in the beginning of 2007 as an operating system made by Apple for its iPhone, while After, it became the default system for the iPod Touch and iPad tablet with a modified version of the interface's latest metrics. The system is one of the operating systems that is a family of Mac OS X.

Windows Phone **Windows Phone** (WP): is a discontinued family of mobile operating systems developed by Microsoft for smartphones as the replacement successor to Windows Mobile and Zune. Windows Phone featured a new user interface derived from Metro design language. Unlike Windows Mobile, it was primarily aimed at the consumer market rather than the enterprise market.

5.2 Mobile Programming Languages

Before you choose the language that you will program your application on, first you must define the operating system of the phone. Popular mobile phones are divided into three operating systems or environments: Android, IOS, and Windows. Everyone has their own languages, for example: The applications running on the Android system are programmed in Java and Kotlin. As for the IOS system, it uses the Swift. As for the Windows system, it uses C# language.

Note, Microsoft provided a beautiful service through which you can program an application that works on all operating systems that are different in C# language with the xamarin platform.

 **java** platform: It is a number of programs and specifications by Sun Microsystems, which together constitute a system for developing and deploying application programs operating in a cross-platform environment. Java is widely used on many types of computer platforms ranging from embedded systems to mobile devices to giant servers and super computers. Java is widely spread in mobile phones,

web servers and integrated systems and is less prevalent in desktop computers. Java applets are used for the web to improve Performance and functionality increase.

 **Kotlin**: It is an Object Oriented programming language that works on the Java platform and can also be run on the JavaScript language platform. The language has been developed by a group of programmers at the Getbrainz Company which is based in Saint Petersburg, Russia - as the name of the language is inspired by the island of Kotlin near the city - the same company that developed Android Studio the official tool for developing Android  applications. Kotlin has been designed to handle fully compatibility with Java, a JDK development package and code library, and allows programming code with fewer lines, faster and more efficiently compared to Java, as it is similar to the Swift language from Apple.

Swift: is a programming language for iOS and OSX operating systems designed by Apple and presented at the Apple Worldwide Developers Conference 2014. The language enables developers to program faster and with minimal errors. The language works perfectly in accordance with the

Cocao and Cocao Touch environments, on which all major iOS devices and Mac system applications are built upon them. With this new language, the company aspires to replace the C-object language which is currently the official programming language for developing applications for Apple products.

 With C# you can use **Xamarin** tools to write native Android, iOS and Windows apps with local user interfaces and share code across multiple platforms, including Windows and macOS.

 **C#**: (Pronounced C-Sharp) is a multi-pattern programming language that enjoys being static, command, definitive, functional, procedural, general, object-oriented (purpose-oriented) (using rows) and is also subject to principles of structured-oriented programming. Microsoft developed this language as part of its development of dot net and has been approved by Ecma (Ecma-334) and International Organization for Standardization (ISO / IEC 23270: 2006). CC Sharp is one of the programming languages designed to

work on the common programming languages infrastructure (CLI). C-Sharp is designed to be simple, modern, general-purpose and object-oriented language. Anders Hilsberg led the development team.

Before designing your application on Android, you need to download the Android Studio program from its official website, and also java SE (jdk). I recommend using the latest software update, due to the periodic update of the program, language, and its libraries. Now we open the Android Studio program, and we start designing our program.

In this tutorial we will design the calculator in Android studio. The buttons included should be: Number Keys: "1", "2", "3", "4", "5", "6", "7", "8", "9", "0". And operation Keys:

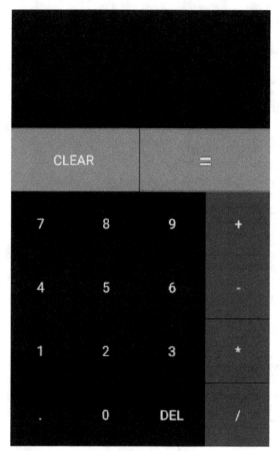

"+", "-", "*", "/" other Keys: "=", "CLEAR". Here the "CLEAR" key should clear out the screen and everything in the memory. The "=" key should apply the operation and give the result. Additional the calculator will have a "DEL" key which is the same as the "backspace" and will remove the last character on the screen. A "." key should show a decimal.

Click on "Start a new Android Studio project

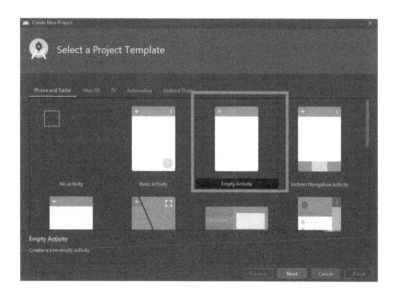

After that we choose "Empty Activity" , the click on "Next",

In configure page, we well writing our project in "Name" field. In "Package name" you are free to change or leave it. But you should know that it is very important when you want to upload your app in Google play, then in "Language" field you can choice java or kotlin language. The "Minimum SDK" you will specify the version it is running on, meaning if you specify V. 16 and the device is V. 15, your app will not run on it, your app will run on devices from V. 16 and above. Then click on "Finish",

This is our screen has opened, now and before anything insert the expression builder library inside the Gradle "bulid.gradle (Module: app)"

implementation 'net.objecthunter:exp4j:0.4.8'

5.3.1 MainActivity.kt

First, we appending 1, 2, 3,.....0 when the we press the keys to the text view, respectively. To do this, we have created a function called evaluateExpression() which does the appending job to the text view. Then in the Equals function, we using the Expression Builder library and calling its method Expression Builder to do the calculations.

package com.drengmr.calculator

import androidx.appcompat.app.AppCompatActivity
import android.os.Bundle
import android.view.Window
import kotlinx.android.synthetic.main.activity_main.*

```kotlin
import net.objecthunter.exp4j.Expression
import net.objecthunter.exp4j.ExpressionBuilder

class MainActivity : AppCompatActivity()
{

    override fun onCreate(savedInstanceState: Bundle?)
    {
        super.onCreate(savedInstanceState)
        //Remove title bar
        getSupportActionBar()?.hide()

        setContentView(R.layout.activity_main)


        /*Number Buttons*/

        tvOne.setOnClickListener {
            evaluateExpression("1", clear = true)
        }

        tvTwo.setOnClickListener {
            evaluateExpression("2", clear = true)
        }

        tvThree.setOnClickListener {
            evaluateExpression("3", clear = true)
        }
        tvFour.setOnClickListener {
            evaluateExpression("4", clear = true)
        }

        tvFive.setOnClickListener {
            evaluateExpression("5", clear = true)
        }

        tvSix.setOnClickListener {
            evaluateExpression("6", clear = true)
        }

        tvSeven.setOnClickListener {
            evaluateExpression("7", clear = true)
        }

        tvEight.setOnClickListener {
            evaluateExpression("8", clear = true)
        }
```

141

```kotlin
tvNine.setOnClickListener {
    evaluateExpression("9", clear = true)
}

tvZero.setOnClickListener {
    evaluateExpression("0", clear = true)
}

/*Operators*/

tvPlus.setOnClickListener {
    evaluateExpression("+", clear = true)
}

tvMinus.setOnClickListener {
    evaluateExpression("-", clear = true)
}

tvMul.setOnClickListener {
    evaluateExpression("*", clear = true)
}

tvDivide.setOnClickListener {
    evaluateExpression("/", clear = true)
}

tvDot.setOnClickListener {
    evaluateExpression(".", clear = true)
}

tvClear.setOnClickListener {
    tvExpression.text = ""
    tvResult.text = ""
}

tvEquals.setOnClickListener {
    val text = tvExpression.text.toString()
    val expression = ExpressionBuilder(text).build()

    val result = expression.evaluate()
    val longResult = result.toLong()
    if (result == longResult.toDouble()) {
        tvResult.text = longResult.toString()
    } else {
        tvResult.text = result.toString()
    }
```

```kotlin
        }

    tvBack.setOnClickListener {
        val text = tvExpression.text.toString()
        if(text.isNotEmpty()) {
            tvExpression.text = text.drop(1)
        }

        tvResult.text = ""
    }
}

/*Function to calculate the expressions using expression builder library*/

fun evaluateExpression(string: String, clear: Boolean) {
    if(clear) {
        tvResult.text = ""
        tvExpression.append(string)
    } else {
        tvExpression.append(tvResult.text)
        tvExpression.append(string)
        tvResult.text = ""
    }
}
}
```

5.3.2   activity_main.xml

This is the main layout file here you need not use the UI editor, rather you can code the entire layout using XML.

```xml
<?xml version="1.0" encoding="utf-8"?>
<LinearLayout xmlns:android="http://schemas.android.com/apk/res/android"
    xmlns:app="http://schemas.android.com/apk/res-auto"
    xmlns:tools="http://schemas.android.com/tools"
    android:layout_width="match_parent"
    android:layout_height="match_parent"
    tools:context=".MainActivity"
    android:background="@android:color/black"
    android:orientation="vertical">

    <TextView
        android:id="@+id/tvExpression"
```

143

```xml
    android:layout_width="match_parent"
    android:layout_height="80dp"
    android:textColor="@color/actionButton"
    android:layout_gravity="end"
    android:ellipsize="start"
    android:singleLine="true"
    android:textSize="40sp"/>


<TextView
    android:id="@+id/tvResult"
    android:layout_width="match_parent"
    android:layout_height="100dp"
    android:textColor="@color/white"
    android:layout_gravity="end"
    android:ellipsize="end"
    android:singleLine="true"
    android:textSize="30sp"/>


<LinearLayout
    android:layout_width="match_parent"
    android:layout_height="match_parent"
    android:orientation="vertical">

    <LinearLayout
        android:layout_width="match_parent"
        android:layout_height="0dp"
        android:layout_weight="1"
        android:orientation="horizontal">
        <TextView
            android:id="@+id/tvClear"
            style="@style/ActionButtonStyle"
            android:text="CLEAR"/>

        <TextView
            android:id="@+id/tvEquals"
            style="@style/EqualButtonStyle"
            android:text="="/>

    </LinearLayout>

    <LinearLayout
        android:layout_width="match_parent"
        android:layout_height="0dp"
        android:layout_weight="1"
```

```xml
    android:orientation="horizontal">

    <TextView
        android:id="@+id/tvSeven"
        style="@style/NumberButtonStyle"
        android:text="7"/>

    <TextView
        android:id="@+id/tvEight"
        style="@style/NumberButtonStyle"
        android:text="8"/>

    <TextView
        android:id="@+id/tvNine"
        style="@style/NumberButtonStyle"
        android:text="9"/>

    <TextView
        android:id="@+id/tvPlus"
        style="@style/NumberActionButton2"
        android:text="+"/>

</LinearLayout>

<LinearLayout
    android:layout_width="match_parent"
    android:layout_height="0dp"
    android:layout_weight="1"
    android:orientation="horizontal">

    <TextView
        android:id="@+id/tvFour"
        style="@style/NumberButtonStyle"
        android:text="4"/>

    <TextView
        android:id="@+id/tvFive"
        style="@style/NumberButtonStyle"
        android:text="5"/>

    <TextView
        android:id="@+id/tvSix"
        style="@style/NumberButtonStyle"
        android:text="6"/>

    <TextView
        android:id="@+id/tvMinus"
```

```xml
        style="@style/NumberActionButton2"
        android:text="-"/>


</LinearLayout>

<LinearLayout
    android:layout_width="match_parent"
    android:layout_height="0dp"
    android:layout_weight="1"
    android:orientation="horizontal">

    <TextView
        android:id="@+id/tvOne"
        style="@style/NumberButtonStyle"
        android:text="1"/>

    <TextView
        android:id="@+id/tvTwo"
        style="@style/NumberButtonStyle"
        android:text="2"/>

    <TextView
        android:id="@+id/tvThree"
        style="@style/NumberButtonStyle"
        android:text="3"/>

    <TextView
        android:id="@+id/tvMul"
        style="@style/NumberActionButton2"
        android:text="*"/>



</LinearLayout>

<LinearLayout
    android:layout_width="match_parent"
    android:layout_height="0dp"
    android:layout_weight="1"
    android:orientation="horizontal">

    <TextView
        android:id="@+id/tvDot"
        style="@style/NumberButtonStyle"
        android:text="."/>
```

146

```xml
    <TextView
        android:id="@+id/tvZero"
        style="@style/NumberButtonStyle"
        android:text="0"/>

    <TextView
        android:id="@+id/tvBack"
        style="@style/NumberButtonStyle"
        android:text="DEL"/>

    <TextView
        android:id="@+id/tvDivide"
        style="@style/NumberActionButton2"
        android:text="/"/>


    </LinearLayout>

</LinearLayout>


</LinearLayout>
```

5.3.3   styles

we can define the format or the look for a UI for calcolator.

```xml
<resources>

    <!-- Base application theme. -->
    <style name="AppTheme"
parent="Theme.AppCompat.Light.DarkActionBar">
        <!-- Customize your theme here. -->
        <item name="colorPrimary">@color/colorPrimary</item>
        <item name="colorPrimaryDark">@color/colorPrimaryDark</item>
        <item name="colorAccent">@color/colorAccent</item>
    </style>
    <!-- ActionButtonStyle for keys "CLEAR" and "/". -->
    <style name="ActionButtonStyle">
        <item name="android:layout_width">0dp</item>
        <item name="android:layout_height">match_parent</item>
        <item name="android:layout_weight">1</item>
        <item name="android:background">@color/actionButton</item>
```

```xml
        <item name = "android:textSize">21sp</item>
        <item name="android:textColor">@android:color/white</item>
        <item name="android:gravity">center</item>
        <item name="android:layout_margin">0.5dp</item>

    </style>
```

<!-- NumberButtonStyle for keys "1, 2, 3, 4, 5, 6, 7, 8, 9, 0". -->
```xml
    <style name="NumberButtonStyle">
        <item name="android:layout_width">0dp</item>
        <item name="android:layout_height">match_parent</item>
        <item name="android:layout_weight">1</item>
        <item name="android:background">@color/numberActionButton</item>
        <item name = "android:textSize">21sp</item>
        <item name="android:textColor">@android:color/white</item>
        <item name="android:gravity">center</item>
        <item name="android:layout_margin">0.5dp</item>
    </style>
```

<!-- EqualButtonStyle for key "=". -->
```xml
    <style name="EqualButtonStyle">
        <item name="android:layout_width">0dp</item>
        <item name="android:layout_height">match_parent</item>
        <item name="android:layout_weight">1</item>
        <item name="android:background">@color/equalButton</item>
        <item name = "android:textSize">40sp</item>
        <item name="android:textColor">@android:color/white</item>
        <item name="android:gravity">center</item>
        <item name="android:layout_margin">0.5dp</item>
    </style>
```

<!-- NumberActionButton2 for keys "*", "-", "+". -->
```xml
    <style name="NumberActionButton2">
        <item name="android:layout_width">0dp</item>
        <item name="android:layout_height">match_parent</item>
        <item name="android:layout_weight">1</item>
        <item
name="android:background">@color/numberActionButton2</item>
        <item name = "android:textSize">21sp</item>
        <item name="android:textColor">@android:color/white</item>
        <item name="android:gravity">center</item>
        <item name="android:layout_margin">0.5dp</item>
    </style>
</resources>
```

148

5.3.4 colors

we can specify the colors for all the buttons of the calculator.

```xml
<?xml version="1.0" encoding="utf-8"?>
<resources>
    <color name="colorPrimary">#6200EE</color>
    <color name="colorPrimaryDark">#3700B3</color>
    <color name="colorAccent">#03DAC5</color>
    <color name = "white">#ffffff</color>
    <color name = "actionButton">#808080</color>
    <color name = "equalButton">#FF0000</color>
    <color name="numberActionButton">#000000</color>
    <color name = "numberActionButton2">#373737</color>
</resources>
```

Note: you can download source code from my github: *https://github.com/mrenarco* and you can know more details on any code on https://developer.android.com/reference.

The term artificial intelligence first appeared in 1956, but has become more popular today, thanks to increased data volumes and advanced algorithms. He focused on topics such as AI research, problem solving and symbolic methods in the 1950s. In the 1960s, the U.S. Department of Defense began training computers to mimic basic human functions, involving such work. For example, the Defense Advanced Research Projects Agency (DARPA); Siri produced smart personal assistants in 2003, long before Alexa or Cortana. This early work paved the way for decision support systems and intelligent search systems that can be designed to complement and strengthen the human capabilities we see in computers today. While Hollywood films and science fiction novels portray AI as human-like robots that take over the world, AI was developed to bring many benefits to the industry.

We can define artificial intelligence as designing the human brain in a machine and providing this machine's ability to "reason, present information, plan, learn, perceive, move and manipulate. Artificial intelligence research can be divided into two main subfields: Robotics and Machine learning. Robotics deals with design, construction, operation and robot use. Machine learning that we focus on is a field of computer science that uses statistical techniques to provide computer systems with functions such as "reasoning, information presentation, planning and learning.

6.1 Fields of Artificial Intelligence

Entertainment: While sitting on your sofa in the future, you can order a special movie that includes the virtual actors of your choice. Advanced forecasting programs, on the other hand, can predict the box office potential while analyzing the story of a movie script.

Medicine: Artificial intelligence algorithms will enable doctors and hospitals to better analyze data and customize healthcare to each patient's genes, environment, and lifestyle. From diagnosing brain tumors to deciding which cancer treatment is best for an individual, AI will drive the personalized medical revolution.

Cyber Security: Companies struggle to stay one step ahead of hackers. USC experts say that self-learning and automation capabilities provided by AI can protect data more systematically and affordably and keep people safer than terrorism or smaller identity theft.

Vital Missions: AI assistants will help people who need their help by age to stay independent and live longer in their own home. Artificial intelligence tools; it will keep nutritious food ready, securely reach objects on high shelves, and monitor people's movements at home.

Transportation: Cars are the point where AI can have the greatest impact in the near future. Unlike people, AI drivers; he never looks at the radio or argues with his children in the back seat. Thanks to Google, the autonomous vehicles used today are expected to increase their use by 2030.

Artificial Intelligence and Tourism: Artificial Intelligence and Tourism virtual assistants, specially developed for tourism and cultural protection regions, meet the expectations of tourists by increasing visitor satisfaction from the beginning to the end of visit, entertainment, travel, event and similar holiday actions. In this way, people can get up-to-date information about visit points such as works, restaurants, services and events belonging to the relevant touristic region, or watch related promotional videos, and they can reach any point they want to go within the scope of touristic areas with navigation guidance.

Artificial Intelligence and Customer Service: Thanks to the Artificial Intelligence and Customer Service experience, users can get information about available products and online technical assistance and even create a technical service appointment. Artificial Intelligence Smart Customer Assistants can be activated by voice or text by imitating human intelligence and natural speech. When they contact you with a voice command system, they can interpret your voice and provide counseling that suits your questions.

Artificial Intelligence and Airport: With the Artificial Intelligence Airport experience, users can learn the flights from the starting point to the destination point together with their prices, track the current flight status using the flight number, and reach the point they want to go to within the airport with indoor navigation guidance.

Artificial Intelligence and Smart Cities: Artificial Intelligence and Smart Cities technologies, which enable municipal services to be performed more efficiently with less cost, enable more effective service delivery to citizens. Smart cities add value to human life and improve the quality of life. Smart city applications that are being used in many municipalities; It focuses more on the areas of environment, transportation, governance, security, health and geographic information systems.

Artificial Intelligence and E-commerce: Artificial Intelligence technologies are used in E-commerce sites to make search consoles private. Artificial intelligence combines information such as customers' shopping habits and interests, and makes it possible for consumers to offer personalized product recommendations. In this way, users are also directed to the website. Artificial intelligence is used for purposes such as offering different discounts to different customers in the e-commerce sector or showing different products to different customers.

Artificial Intelligence and Activities: Artificial Intelligence and Activity Assistants; It allows users to get up-to-date information on events, motion pictures and more, or to watch promotional videos on the topic. In addition to this; It offers the opportunity to review weather and traffic conditions, check promotions in cafes and shops, and learn about current campaigns.

Artificial Intelligence and Banking and Financial Services: Artificial Intelligence and Banking and Financial Services experience assists investors on many topics ranging from account transactions to stock proposals by increasing the business efficiency of users. In order for you to use the time allocated for stock tracking, trading process, fund tracking and similar processes more effectively; it allows you to get information about user account information, credit information, updates, investment reports and more, and it monitors this process for you.

Artificial Intelligence and Education: Artificial Intelligence and Education technologies are able to design the program that it will create in accordance with the individual, as it can analyze students' missing areas. It is anticipated that students will be more productive and provide added value to their environment as an individual who loves their job in the future with the personally created education program. Artificial intelligence, which personalizes educational software according to student needs, understands the shortcomings of students better and creates personalized support advantage for development. Intelligent data collection, supported by intelligent computer systems, is a process that is actively implemented by many schools today. Today, some schools use artificial intelligence technology to keep track of students' progress and improve student performance with this analysis.

6.2   Intuitive (heuristics) Problem Solving

The computerization of intuitive human-like processes has been problematic thus far. The main challenge is that intuition is driven by irrational logic, while most models of artificial intelligence are governed by logic. Some scientists do not believe that such intrinsic human ability as intuition can be implemented at all in artificial intelligent factors. For example, Dreyfus insisted that "humans have an axiom intelligence that" thinking "machines cannot simply be matched" (Dreyfus & Dreyfus, 1986); In the opinion of Roger Penrose (1989) mind cannot be an algorithm. And John Searle (1990) asserted that "programs are neither author nor sufficient for minds." However, other thinkers are more optimistic about the possibility of electronic processes similar to human processes. Marvin Minsky believed computers would do the programmed things that humans would do, and Newell and Simon predicted that properly programmed machines could do anything an intelligent person could do (cited in Dreyfus & Dreyfus, 1986).

For example, we will discuss the need and types of inference to solve problems. The seller has a list of cities, and he must visit each of them exactly once. There are direct routes between each pair of cities in the list. Look for the path that the seller must follow for the shortest possible round trip trip that begins and ends in any of the cities.

This is a classic problem with graph theory, which has no closed algorithmic analytical solution. This problem can be solved to get a very short list of cities. But it is disrupted as the number of cities grows. If there are N cities, and the starting point is random if the distance between each pair of cities is the same regardless of travel direction, then there will be N (N-1) paths! / 2 possible. Suppose we have a computer that can list all possible solutions to the problem of 20 cities in one hour.

Then it is clear that it will take 20 hours to use the above formula to solve 21 cities problem and 17.5 days to solve 22 cities problem. The problem of 25 cities will take nearly 6 centuries. Given this phenomenal growth in computing time with a full size count, it's clearly not a start.

This phenomenon is called a combative explosion. Even if the computer is able to process every movement in one millisecond, it will take infinitely long time to reach a solution. This type of search is called a BLIND search. There is no solution to these problems, except for invoking some special types of control strategies where mobility requirements and methodology must be sacrificed. A guaranteed solution was found using HEURISTICS.

6.3   Game theory

Game theory is a branch of mathematics that is used to model strategic interaction between different players in a context with predefined rules and results. Game theory can be applied in a different range of artificial intelligence:

1- Multi-agent artificial intelligence systems.

2- Learn to imitate and reinforce.

3- Training the opponent on obstetric adversarial networks (GANs).

Game theory can also be used to describe many situations in our daily lives and machine learning models (Table 6.1). For example, a rating algorithm such as SVM (Support Vector Machines) can be explained in terms of a two-player game where one of the players challenges the other to find the best level of hyper that gives him the most difficult rating points. The game will then meet a solution that will be a comparison between the strategic abilities of the players (for example, how successful the first player has been in challenging the second player to rank the hard data points and how good the second player is in determining the best decision limits).

Application of game theory	
1. Finance	9. Biology
2. Telecommunications	10. Environment
3. Transport	11. Agriculture
4. Computer systems	12. Political science
5. Sociology	13. Law and ethic
6. Psychology	14. Insurance
7. Hazard, parlor games, and sport	15. War and defence
8. Medicine	16. Business

Table 6.2. Game Theory Applications.

6.3.1   Game Theory Types

Game theory can be divided into 5 main types of games:

1. **Collaborative Games vs Non-Cooperative Games**: In cooperative games, participants can form alliances to increase their chances of winning the game (such as negotiations). In non-cooperative games, participants cannot instead form alliances (such as wars).

2. **Symmetric Games vs Asymmetric Games**: In a symmetric game, all participants have the same goals and their strategies are implemented only to achieve them which will determine who wins the game (such as chess). In asymmetric games instead, participants have different or conflicting goals.

3. **Perfect vs Imperfect Information Games**: In perfect information games, all players can see the movements of other players (such as chess). Instead, in missing information games, the movements of other players (such as card games) are hidden.

4. **Simultaneous Games vs Sequential Games**: In concurrent games, different players can take action simultaneously. Instead, in serial games, each player is familiar with the previous actions of other players (such as board games).

5. **Zero-Sum vs Non-Zero Sum Games**: In Zero Sum games, if a player wins something that causes a loss to other players. In Non-Zero Sum games, instead, many players can take advantage of another player's gains.

6.4   Predicate Logic

Predicate logic is a simple form of logic also known as logic. The proposal contains TRUTH values (0 and 1) which means that it can contain one of two values, i.e. true or false. This is the most used and basic logic. This logic is used to develop robust search algorithms including implementation methods. Mathematically, logical operators combine proposals to make other proposals by following some specific rules.

The predicate logic of artificial intelligence is used for planning, problem solving, smart control and most importantly for decision making. Everything related to logical functions and statements where there are more than just valid and false values, including certainty as well as uncertainty, have led to the foundation of machine learning models. It is a useful tool for thinking, but it has limitations because it cannot see prepositions within it and take advantage of the relationships between them.

Properties

1. Satisfactory: An atomic proposal formula is acceptable if there is a correct explanation.

2. Stuffing: correct suggested formula or correct padding for all possible explanations.

3. Contradiction: The proposed formula is contradictory (unsatisfactory) if there is no correct explanation.

4. Probability: The proposed logic can be conditional, which means that it cannot be padding or inconsistency.

6.5 Logical Programming

It is the main tool for exploring and building computer programs that can be used to simulate smart processes such as learning, thinking, and understanding symbolic information in context. Although in the early days of computer language design, the primary use of computers for calculations using numbers, it was soon also discovered that bit strings can represent not only numbers, but also features of arbitrary objects. Operations on these features or symbols can be used to represent the rules for creating, linking, or manipulating symbols. This led to the concept of symbolic computation as an appropriate means of identifying algorithms that processed information of any kind and could therefore be used to simulate human intelligence. It soon became evident that code-coding required a higher level of abstraction than was possible with these programming languages specifically designed to handle numbers, for example, Fortran.

In artificial intelligence, automation or programming for all aspects of human perception is one of its foundations in cognitive science through the symbolic and semi-symbolic artificial intelligence approach, natural language processing, computer vision, and evolutionary or adaptive systems. It is inherent in the very complex problem area that in the initial stage of programming a specific AI problem, it can only be poorly identified. It is only through interactive and progressive optimization that the most accurate specifications are possible. This is also due to the fact that typical AI problems tend to be very specific in the field, and therefore heuristic strategies must be developed empirically through a generation and testing approach (also known as fast-fast writing). In this way, AI programming is markedly different from standard software engineering approaches as programming usually begins from detailed formal specifications. In AI programming, the implementation effort is actually part of the problem identification process.

6.5.1   Lisp Programming Language

Lisp is the first functional programming language: it was invented to support symbolic computation using linked lists like Central Data Structure (Lisp means list processor). John McCarthy notes that the methods of flow control of mathematical functions - recursive and conditional - are suitable theoretical methods for performing symbolic computations. Moreover, the concepts of functional abstraction and functional application defined in the Lambda account provide the necessary high-level abstraction required to identify problems of artificial intelligence.

Lisp was invented by McCarthy in 1958 and the first version of the Lisp programming environment was available in 1960 and it consists of a translator, translator and dynamic memory allocation and allocation mechanisms (known as garbage collection). A year later, the first language standard, called Lisp 1.5, was introduced. Since then a number of Lisp dialects and programming environments have been developed, for example, MacLisp, FranzLisp, InterLisp, Common Lisp and Scheme. Although they differ in some specific details, their grammatical and semantic essence is essentially the same. This is the essence that we would like to present in this overview. Lisp's most used dialects are Lisp and Scheme. In this article we have chosen Common Lisp to present various aspects of Lisp with concrete examples. However, examples can be easily adapted to other Lisp dialects.

6.5.2   Prolog Programming Language

In the 1970s, an alternative model of symbolic computation and artificial intelligence programming arose from success in the field of proving spontaneous theory. It is worth noting that Robinson's (1965) accuracy confirmation procedure demonstrated that formal logic, especially the original calculus, can be used as a symbol for identifying algorithms, and thus for performing symbolic calculations. In the early 1970s, Prolog (a shortcut to programming in logic), the first logical programming language appeared. It was developed by Alain Colmerauer, Robert Kowalski and Phillippe Roussel. Essentially, Prolog consists of a method for identifying the original calculus proposals and a restricted form of decision. Prolog programming consists of defining facts about objects and their relationships, and rules that define their logical relationships. Prolog programs are introductory sets of statements about a problem because they do not determine how the result is calculated, but rather the logical structure of the result. This is quite different from deterministic and even functional programming, where the focus is on determining how the result is calculated. With Prolog, programming can be done at a very abstract level very close to the official specification of the problem. Prolog is still the most important logical programming language. There are a number of commercial programming systems on the market that include modern programming units, i.e. translator tools, proofreader and visualization. Prolog has been successfully used in a number of areas of artificial intelligence such as expert systems and natural language processing, but also in areas such as relational database management systems or in education.

6.6 Expert Systems

After the dawn of modern computers in the late 1940's - early 1950's, researchers began to realize the enormous potential that these machines possessed for modern society. One of the first challenges was to make this machine capable of "thinking" like humans. In particular, they make these machines capable of making important decisions as humans do. The medical and healthcare field presented a puzzling challenge to enable these machines to make medical diagnostic decisions.

Thus, in the late 1950s, after the information age had fully arrived, researchers began to experiment with the potential for using computer technology to simulate human decision-making. For example, biomedical researchers have begun creating computer aided systems for diagnostic applications in medicine and biology. These early diagnostic systems used patient symptoms and laboratory test results as inputs to generate diagnostic results. These systems are often described as the early forms of expert systems. However, researchers have realized that there are significant

166

limitations when using traditional methods such as matching statistical patterns of flow charts, or probability theory.

Expert System is a computer program designed to solve complex problems and provide decision-making ability like a human expert. It does this by extracting knowledge from its knowledge base using inference and reasoning rules according to user queries.

The expert system is part of artificial intelligence, and the first ES was developed in 1970, which was the first successful approach to artificial intelligence. It solves the most complex problem as an expert by extracting the knowledge stored in its knowledge base. The system assists in making compsex problems using both facts and inference as a human expert. It is called that because it contains experts' knowledge of a particular field and can solve any complex problem in this specific field. These systems are designed for a specific field, such as medicine, science, etc.

The performance of the expert system depends on the knowledge of the expert stored in his knowledge base. The more knowledge stored in the knowledge base, the better the performance of the system. A common example of ES is suggesting spelling mistakes as you type in the Google search box.

6.6.1 Characteristics of Expert Systems

High performance
Understandable
Reliable
Highly responsive

6.6.2 Building blocks of expert systems

Each expert system consists of two main parts: the knowledge base. Logic, or reasoning, the engine.

The knowledge base for expert systems contains both factual and instructional knowledge. Realistic knowledge is that knowledge of a widely shared task area, which is usually found in textbooks or magazines, and is generally agreed upon by those with knowledge in a particular field.

Guidance knowledge is less rigorous, more experienced, and more judgmental knowledge of performance. In contrast to real knowledge, exploratory knowledge is rarely discussed, and it is largely individual. It is knowledge of good practice, good judgment, and reasonable thinking in this field. It is the knowledge that underlies "the art of good guessing".

Knowledge representation formalizes and organizes knowledge. One of the widely used representations is the production base, or simply the base. The rule is made up of the IF part and then the part (also called condition and procedure). The IF section lists a set of conditions in some logical combination. The piece of knowledge represented by the production base is related to the logic line that is developed if the IF part of the rule is met; Thus, THEN can be terminated, or problem-solving actions can be taken. Expert systems whose knowledge is represented in the form of a rule called rule-based systems.

Another widely used representation, called unit (also known as frame, chart, or list structure) is based on a more negative view of knowledge. A unit is a set of symbolic knowledge associated with the entity to be represented. Typically, the unit consists of a list of entity properties and associated values.

Since each task field consists of many entities standing in different relationships, properties can also be used to define relationships, and the values of these properties are the names of other related units according to the relationships. One unit can also represent knowledge that is a "special case" for another unit, or some units can be "parts of" another unit.

A problem solving model, or model, organizes steps that are taken to solve and control a problem. One popular but robust model includes the IF-THEN rule sequence to form a line of reasoning. If the chain starts from a set of conditions and moves toward some conclusions, then the method is called sequencing forward. If the conclusion is known (for example, a goal to be achieved) but the path to this conclusion is unknown, then backward thinking is required, and the method is sequenced backward. These problem-solving methods are incorporated into program modules called inference engines or inferential knowledge-based procedures that use them in the knowledge base to form a line of reasoning.

The expert's knowledge base is what he learned in school, from colleagues, and from years of experience. It is assumed that the more his experience, the more his store of knowledge. Knowledge allows him to interpret information in his databases to benefit from diagnosis, design and analysis.

Although the expert system consists mainly of a knowledge base and reasoning engine, there are other features worth noting: thinking with uncertainty, and explaining the logic line.

Knowledge is always incomplete and uncertain. To deal with uncertain knowledge, the base may have been associated with it as a confidence or weight factor. A set of methods for using uncertain knowledge with uncertain data in the inference process is called inference with uncertainty. There is an important subcategory of thinking with uncertainty called "fuzzy logic", and the systems that use it are known as "fuzzy systems".

Since the expert system uses unconfirmed or exploratory knowledge (as we humans do), its reliability is often questioned (as is the case with humans). When the answer to a problem is questionable, we tend to know the rationale. If the rationale appears plausible, we tend to believe the answer. This is the case with expert systems. Most expert systems have the ability to answer model questions: "Why answer X?" Explanations can be created by tracing the logic line used by the inference engine (Feigenbaum, McCorduck et al. 1988).

Knowledge is the most important component of any expert system. The strength of expert systems lies in the specific, high-quality knowledge they contain about mission areas. Artificial Intelligence researchers will continue to explore and add to the current collection of knowledge representation and thinking. But in knowledge lies power. Given the importance of knowledge in expert systems and because the current way of acquiring knowledge is slow and boring, much of the future of expert systems depends on breaking the bottleneck in acquiring knowledge and in codifying and representing a large knowledge infrastructure.

6.6.3 Examples of Expert Systems

Following are examples of Expert Systems

MYCIN: It was based on backward chaining and could identify various bacteria that could cause acute infections. It could also recommend drugs based on the patient's weight.

DENDRAL: Expert system used for chemical analysis to predict molecular structure.

PXDES: Expert system used to predict the degree and type of lung cancer

CaDet: Expert system that could identify cancer at early stages

6.7 Natural Language Processing

Natural Language Processing (NLP) is the field of computer science and linguistics concerned with interactions between computers and natural languages. Which started as a branch of artificial intelligence which in turn branched from informatics,

There is controversy over the convergence and variance of natural language processing from the field of computational linguistics. Computational Linguistics has defined computational linguistics as focusing on the theoretical aspects of natural language processing. Modern algorithms are based on natural language processing in machine learning, especially statistical machine learning. Recent research into statistical machine learning algorithms requires an understanding of a number of disparate areas, including linguistics, computer science, and statistics.

The first systems such as SHRDLU, which worked in a specific environment of words, worked very effectively, which led researchers to the extreme optimism that quickly faded when systems were applied in more realistic environments with complexity and thumb (lack of clarity) in the languages people use.

Understanding natural languages is sometimes referred to as the whole problem of artificial intelligence, because the distinction and understanding of natural languages requires extensive knowledge of the outside world and the ability to control it. Defining the concept of "understanding" is one of the main problems in addressing natural languages.

An example of some problems facing systems of understanding and analyzing natural languages:

The phrase "We gave the banana monkeys because they were hungry" and the sentence "We gave the banana monkeys because they were mature" for them with the same grammatical composition, but the pronoun "because" is in a word because it comes in the first on the monkeys, and in the second it returns to the banana: so understanding the sentence correctly is not possible without Knowing the properties of bananas and the behavior of monkeys.

The beginning of this phase (circa 1970 AD) was associated with the loss of hope that an entire language could be represented within the computer and researchers limited their efforts to specific language structures closely related to semantic analysis tests. The first two programs to demonstrate this change were the Shrdlu a Lingrad and Lunar Wood. This stage is also characterized by limiting the fear of understanding to single sentences without trying to link these sentences with a full text.

The complete program of natural language processing is usually organized in the form of an algorithm, in which ovals represent the information to be processed, and rectangles include subprogrammes that lead to the required conversions between these shapes.

As there is no general agreement on what the internal representation should contain or what the meaning of the sentence is, the division of natural language processing into subprogrammes is completely optional, so the conclusion process can begin before the end of the analysis process. Moreover, it is not necessarily that each program contains Heuristic steps.

Usually, a program that uses natural language to extract information from the database is required to extract the correct information, but there may be a more advanced program to interpret ambiguous inquiries. Researchers like Coulon and Kayser prefer the concept of interpretation with different degrees of depth over internal representation.

6.7.1   Levels of natural language analysis

As for the written texts, their dissolution passes in several stages that differ according to the method of analysis and language singing. For example, the treatment of the Arabic language requires analysis that includes all levels. The most common levels of analysis follow the stages:

Morphological analysis

He analyzes the word to know its root and its morphological weight and the increase, decrease, reason, substitution, slurring, or heart that occurred in it, in addition to knowing the precedents and type of these precedents, and the subsequent pronouns or suffixes and components of those pronouns and suffixes, and knowing the type of the word itself ; Name, verb, letter, to other morphological descriptions that pertain to each section of the Arabic word.

Grammar analysis

It is the part that deals with the relationship of words to each other, the structure of the sentence, and other grammatical information, and depends on the morphological stage.

Semantic analysis

It is the part that is concerned with understanding the intended meaning of the sentence by logically linking the topic of the conversation in the sentence with information from the real world.

6.8 Pattern Recognition

Pattern recognition is one of the branches of machine learning and generally artificial intelligence, and research and techniques for this science aim to find or develop techniques to identify specific patterns or structures in digital signals, where the signal can represent an image that contains a written letter, a musical phrase, or a syllable that represents A word or even a computer text, and the pattern to be recognized may be the letter in which the image or instrument is used in the syllable or the word pronounced in the syllable or determine whether the computer text speaks of physics, literature or politics ...

6.8.1 General structure of the model recognition systems

Data Acquisition: The income that we want to know is obtained from the user.

Signal preprocessing: At this point we remove noise from the signal and convert it into a regular form using Scaling and other simple operations. The goal is to get a "clean" signal that makes it easier for the rest of the stages to work.

Feature Extraction: At this stage, traits and characteristics of the signal are created that help define the model (s) they represent.

For example, in the field of speech recognition, the linguistic information in the sign determines the word, not the information that identifies the speaker or his psychological state. If we can accurately extract the linguistic information, the identification becomes easier (as we have deleted other information that is not useful in the identification). Linguistic information cannot easily be separated, so we perform a set of operations that help in this and then calculate a set of values that define the desired word and the different these values for stored models, the more detailed the extraction, if distinguishing between them becomes easy.

Classification: Here the income is a characteristic beam, and we have to determine which of the stored models this beam represents. There are many techniques, such as neural networks, etc.

6.8.2 Applications

Writing recognition: Recognizing characters in an image that contains writing and converting it into computer text

Speech recognition: Speech recognition is spoken in an audio text and converted into computer text

Get to know the speaker: Find out who is the person who is speaking in an audio clip (among a group of people whose system maintains audio clips (a form) of their words).

6.9 Artificial Neural Networks

Artificial neural networks (ANNs) is an information technology developed by inspiring the information processing technique of the human brain. With ANN, the way the simple biological nervous system works is imitated. In other words, it is the digital modeling of biological neuron cells and the synaptic bond that these cells establish with each other. Neurons form networks by connecting to each other in various ways. These networks are capable of learning, storing and revealing the relationship between data. In other words, ANNs produce solutions to problems that normally require a person's natural abilities to think and observe. The main reason why a person can produce solutions for the problems that require thinking and observation skills is the ability of the human brain and hence the ability to learn by living or trying.

Learning in biological systems is by adjusting synaptic connections between neurons. In other words, people go through a learning process by living from birth. During this process, the brain is constantly developing. As you live and experience, synaptic connections are set and even new connections are created. In this way, learning takes place. This also applies to ANN. Learning happens by using examples through education; In other words, realization occurs by processing input / output data, that is, the training algorithm adjusts the weights of the synapses repeatedly using this data until a convergence is achieved.

ANNs are mathematical systems consisting of many processing units (neurons) that are weighted together. A processing unit is actually an equation often referred to as the transfer function. This processing unit receives signals from other neurons; it combines, transforms and produces a numerical result. In general, the processing units roughly correspond to real neurons and are connected in a network; this structure also forms neural networks.

At the center of neural computing are distributed, adaptive and nonlinear processing concepts. ANNs operate differently than traditional processors. In conventional processors, a single central processing unit performs each movement in turn. ANNs are made up of a number of simple trading units, each dealing with a part of a major problem. In the simplest way, a processing unit weighs an input with a set of weights, converts it nonlinearly and generates an output value. At first glance, the way units work is misleadingly simple. The power of neural computation comes from the dense linking structure of the process units that share the total processing load. In these systems, healthier learning is provided by back propagation method.

In most ANNs, neurons with similar characteristics are constructed in layers and transfer functions are run simultaneously. Almost all networks have neurons that receive data and neurons that produce output.

Mathematical function, the main element of ANN, is shaped by the architecture of the network. To put it more clearly, the basic structure of the function is determined by the size of the weights and the way the process elements operate. The behavior of ANNs, that is, how they relate input data to output data, is first affected by the transfer functions of neurons, how they are connected and the weight of these connections.

Besides the advantages of artificial neural networks, there are some drawbacks. These drawbacks can be listed as follows:

It is not known what happened in the system.
Stability analysis cannot be performed except for some networks.

It can be difficult to apply to different systems.

The fuzzy logic is a form of logic, used in some expert systems and applications of artificial intelligence. This logic was created in 1965 by the Azerbaijani scientist "Lotfi Zada" from the University of California, where he developed it to use it as a better way to process data, but his theory did not receive attention until 1974 where The logic of obscurity was used to regulate a steam engine, and then its applications developed until it reached to manufacture a fuzzy logic chip which was used in many products such as cameras.

There are many motives that motivated scientists to develop fuzzy logic. With the development of computers and software, the desire to invent or program systems that can handle inaccurate human-style information has arisen, but this has created a problem where the computer can only deal with precise and specific data. This approach has resulted in what are known as expert systems or artificial intelligence, and fuzzy logic is one of the theories through which such systems can be built.

fuzzy logic in the broad sense is a logical system based on a generalization of the traditional two-valued logic, in order to infer in unconfirmed circumstances. In a narrow sense, it is theories and techniques that use foggy groups that are unlimited, infinite groups. This logic represents an easy way to describe and represent human experience, as it provides practical solutions to real problems, which are cost effective and reasonable solutions, compared to other solutions that offer other technologies.

6.10.1 Fuzzy Logic Architecture

The structure of fuzzy logic consists of the following components:

Base base

This is the set of rules along with the If-Then terms used to make decisions. However, recent developments in fuzzy logic have reduced the number of rules in the base rule. This set of rules is also called a knowledge base.

Confusion

This is the step where fragile numbers are converted into mysterious groups. A fragile group is a group of elements that have identical properties. Depending on a particular logic, the item can belong to the group or not. Wrinkled groups rely on binary logic - yes or no answers.

Here, error signals and physical values are converted into a natural blur subset. On any Fuzzy Logic system, the fuzzifier separates input signals into five states:

Great positive
Positive average
Small
Average negative
Big negative

The jamming process converts obvious inputs, such as room temperature, that are brought in by the sensors and passed to the control system for further processing. Fuzzy logic control system is based on fuzzy logic. Common household appliances, such as air conditioners and washing machines, have foggy control systems inside.

6.10.2 The advantages of fuzzy logic in artificial intelligence

The benefits of using Fuzzy Logic systems are as follows:

1. It is a robust system where no precise inputs are required

2. These systems are able to accommodate several types of inputs including vague, distorted or inaccurate data

3. If the feedback sensor stops working, you can reprogram it according to the situation

4. Fuzzy logic algorithms can be encoded with less data, so they don't take up much memory

5. Since it resembles human logic, these systems are able to solve complex problems where there are vague inputs and make decisions accordingly

6. These systems are flexible and the rules can be modified

7. The systems have simple structure and can be built easily

8. You can save on system costs as these systems can accommodate cheap sensors

6.10.3 The disadvantages of fuzzy logic in artificial intelligence

Let's take a look at the disadvantages of fuzzy logic systems:

1. The accuracy of these systems has been compromised as the system mostly works on inaccurate data and inputs

2. There is no single systematic approach to solving a problem using fuzzy logic. As a result, many solutions arise to a specific problem, which leads to confusion

3. Because of the inaccuracy of the results, they are not always widely accepted

4. The main disadvantage of fuzzy logic control systems is that they are completely dependent on human knowledge and experience

5. You should update the Fuzzy Logic Control System rules regularly

6. These systems cannot recognize machine learning or neural networks

7. Systems require a lot of tests to verify and verify them

6.11 Evolutionary Methods and Genetic Algorithm

Genetic Algorithms is a method of optimization and research. This method can be classified as one of the methods of evolutionary algorithms that rely on imitating the work of nature from Darwini's perspective.

The genetic algorithm uses research technology to find exact or approximate solutions that optimize. Genetic algorithms are classified as global search heuristics. It is also a specific class of evolutionary algorithms also known as evolutionary computation that uses technology inspired by evolutionary biology such as inheritance, mutation, selection, and crossover.

Genetic algorithms are considered an important technique in searching for the optimal choice from a set of solutions available for a specific design, and they adopt the Darwinian principle of selection where this genetic treatment passes the optimal advantages through successive reproductive

186

processes, and support these characteristics, and these characteristics have the greatest ability to enter the reproductive process , And to produce optimal offspring, and by repeating the genetic cycle, the quality of the offspring will gradually improve.

Evolutionary algorithms is a subset of evolutionary accounts. Evolutionary algorithm uses some mechanisms inspired by biological evolution: cloning, mutation, recombination, and selection. Candidate solutions to the optimal problem play the role of individuals in a segment of the population. The appropriate task determines the environment in which the "life" of the solutions takes place (see also Mathematical Optimization) The evolution of the population takes place after the repeated application of the above process. Artificial evolution describes the individual process that involves evolutionary algorithms; evolutionary algorithm is the individual components that contribute to artificial evolution.

Evolutionary algorithms often perform well to find approximate solutions to all kinds of problems because they ideally do not make any assumption about the appropriate task behind the scene, and this generalization is indicated by the successes achieved in various fields such as engineering, art, biology, economics, marketing, Genetics, research processes, robotics, social sciences, physics, politics and chemistry

Regardless of its usefulness as a mathematics optimizer, evolutionary computation and algorithms have also been used as an experimental framework within which to validate theories about biological evolution and natural selection, particularly by working in the field of [artificial life]. Of the techniques of evolutionary algorithms applied to modeling biological evolution are usually limited to exploration of micro evolutionary processes, but some computer simulations, such as Tierra and Aveda, attempted to model the great evolutionary dynamics.

The existence of many limitations to evolutionary algorithms is likely due to the lack of a clear genetic pattern - to distinguish phenotype. In nature, the fertilized egg cell undergoes a complex process known as the fetus to become mature by phenotype. This indirect coding is needed to make genetic research more powerful (i.e. reduces the possibility of fatal mutations), and may also improve the organism's ability to develop. Recent work in the field of creating an artificial embryo, or artificial development systems, seeks to address these concerns.

6.12 Robotics

Robotics is a branch of artificial intelligence that consists of electrical engineering, mechanical engineering and computer science to design and implement robotics.

Aspects of robots

Robots have a mechanical build, shape, or shape designed to accomplish a certain task.

It contains electrical components that control and control the machines.

It contains a certain level of computer program that determines what, when and how a robot does something.

Difference in robot system and other artificial intelligence program

Robots	AI Programs
They operate in real physical world	They usually operate in computer-stimulated worlds.
Inputs to robots is analog signal in the form of speech waveform or images	The input to an AI program is in symbols and rules.

They need special hardware with sensors and effectors.	They need general purpose computers to operate on.

Robots are created with the following:

1. Power supply - Robots are powered by batteries, solar, hydraulic or pneumatic power sources.

2. Motors - converts energy into motion.

3. Electric motors (AC / DC) - required for rotational motion.

4. Air muscles - approximately 40% shrink when absorbing air in them.

5. Muscle Wires - Shrink by 5% as electrical current passes through them.

6. Piezo Motors and Ultrasonic Motors - the best for industrial robots.

7. Sensors - It provides real-time knowledge of the task environment. Robots are equipped with vision sensors to calculate depth in the environment. The touch sensor mimics the mechanical properties of touch receivers for human finger tips.

The network models used by Ivakhnenko and Lapa in 1965 had many layers of nonlinear features, and algorithms similar to the Deep Learning algorithms used in these networks extracted features using polynomial activation functions analyzed by statistical methods. By selecting statistical methods and selecting the best features, these features were transferred to the next layer. Back propagation was not used in training of networks from one end to the other. By using independent layers for the training of the network, they ensured that the previous layer was aligned with the least squares independent of the next layer. However, this feature extraction used by Ivakhnenko causes an architecture that terminates and decreases as its steps cannot progress further with the addition of other layers.

Deep Learning: It is an artificial intelligence method that uses multi-layered artificial neural networks in areas such as object recognition, speech recognition, and natural language processing, and is one of the types of machine learning. Deep Learning, instead of learning with coded rules different from traditional machine learning methods; They can automatically learn from the icons of data of pictures, videos, sounds and texts. Because they are flexible, they can also learn from raw image or text data and their accuracy can be increased depending on the size of the data. In addition, Deep Learning performs learning through examples. For a problem that the machine is asked to solve, it is sufficient to give a model that enables the solution to solve the problem by evaluating the samples instead of using the rule sets. The machine is expected to perform the learning process by giving a simple command list in order to correct the error in the solution of the problem. Model selection is effective in solving the problem. The model to be determined in accordance with the problem will contribute more to the solution of the problem. The concept of Deep Learning was first introduced in 2006 by Hinton, suggesting that multi-layered artificial neural networks can be trained more efficiently.

7.1 Deep Learning Concepts

7.1.1 Neuron

The neuron that forms the basic structure of the neural network is the basic element of our brain (Figure 7.1). When new information is received, it is processed and then converted to output. In the neural network, an input to the neuron is received, processed, and produces an output or result output sent to other neurons for the next process.

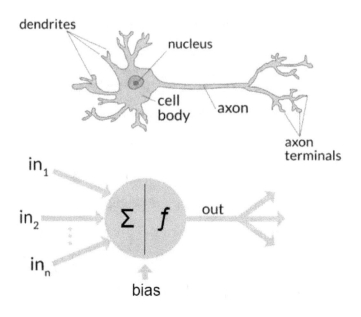

Figure 7.1. Neuron and Artificial Neuron.

7.1.2   Weights

The input is multiplied by a weight when it arrives at the neuron. In a two-input neuron, each neuron input has a weight assigned to that input (Figure 7-2). These randomly launched weights are updated during the training of the model. The higher weight value is given to the inputs considered to be more important after the training by the neural network. However, it can be concluded that an input or property whose zero weight value is given by the neural network is insignificant. Assuming that an entry a is associated with the weight of w1, the entry after passing through the node is expressed as a * w1.

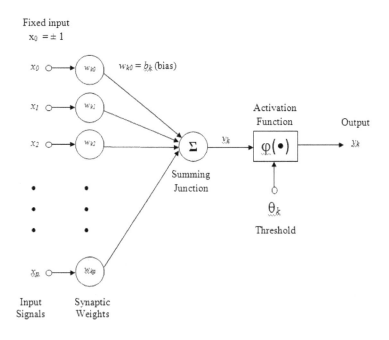

Figure 7.2. Weights in Artificial Neuron.

7.1.3 Deflection

In addition to the weight applied to the input, the additionally applied linear component is called bias or deviation. This deviation is; The weight multiplier is added as the basis for changing the range of the input, which is

194

defined as the input and multiplied by the weight of the input. As a result of adding the deviation value, the input is expressed as a * w1 + bias. This input is the last linear component of its transformation.

7.2   Fundamentals of Deep Learning

Deep feed forward networks, feed forward neural networks and multi-layered perseptrons are the foundations of Deep Learning models. The target in the feed forward network is an F function approach. For the classifier, the F function; It is a map from entry x to category y. The feed forward network defines a mapping for the category y defined by Q parameters and x entries. And it learns the Q parameters that give the best function approach. There is no feedback connection in this network model. If a feedback link is found, this network is referred to as a Repetitive Neural Network. Feed Forward Networks, which are frequently used in machine learning, form the basis of many commercial applications and Wrapped Networks (CNN) are also examples of Feed Forward Network model. Wrapped Nets are Specialized Feed Forward Networks used for picture-to-object recognition. Feedforward Networks are one of the basic steps in the formation of repetitive networks used in natural language processing. Feed Forward Networks, consisting of at least 3 layers in which the functions that make up the layers that can contain different functions in each layer are connected with each other in the chain structure, are expressed as deep networks and they have provided the emergence of Deep Learning. They are referred to as neural networks as they are inspired by neuroscience when creating these networks. Each layer of the network is usually vector-valued. The dimensions of the hidden layers determine the width of the model. It can be interpreted that each vector element plays a role close to neuron. Instead of thinking of the layer as a function that represents a single vector (vector-vector) function, we can think of it as a layer containing several units, each representing a vector-scalar function that moves in parallel. Each unit is similar to a neuron in that it receives input from many other units and calculates these inputs with its own activation value. The use of many vector-valued layers has been removed from neuroscience. The selection of F functions used to calculate vector-valued representations in the layers used was created by observing the calculations of biological neurons observed in neuroscience. While being guided by many disciplines such as modern neural networks, mathematics and engineering, the aim is not a full modeling of the brain.

Feed Forward Networks; instead of functional models of the brain, they are function approach machines that are designed to be successful in statistical generalization with the inference made from known general opinions about the brain. In order to understand Feed Forward Networks, linear models should be looked at first. Linear models such as logistic regression and linear regression can be preferred with convex optimization or because they provide a reliable and effective fit in closed forms. However, since the capacities of linear models are limited by linear functions, they have a certain deficiency. Therefore, these models cannot understand the relationship between both input variables.

7.3   Deep Learning Algorithms

Deep learning algorithms are algorithms that are generally applied to an extremely complex set of definitions such as images, sound sequences and text, and the correct production process basically covers the simulation of the entire universe. Finding the right scale model with the right number of parameters means checking the complexity of the model is not a simple problem. The model that is most suitable for generalization is arranged in a suitable way by minimizing the generalization error. In this way, wide, deep

197

and regular models are produced. Algorithms of Deep Learning methods will be explained in the following sections, both mathematically and in practice. In this section, introduction information to the methods is given.

7.3.1 Convolutional Neural Networks (CNN)

Convolutional (Transformational) Neural Networks (CNN); It is also known as the Customized Transformational Neural Network that processes data, known as the grid topology. In the example that includes time series data, it can also be thought of as a 2D grid of pixels, taking samples and displaying the data by considering them as one-dimensional grid at regular time intervals. CNN are the most popular networks applied to computer vision and sharing the most common parameters within the network. Natural images have many statistical features with fixed translation. For example, by turning a pixel to the right in a cat photo, the cat's picture is not distorted. CNNs account for this feature by sharing parameters corresponding to multiple image positions. The same feature (hidden unit with the same weight) is calculated at different locations of the input. This allows us to find the cat in what position in the image using the same cat detector. If it is defined as convolutional, transformation or fold, it is expressed as a linear process.

198

Alternating Neural Networks are neural networks that use curl or transformation instead of a general matrix multiplication in at least one of its layers. Figure 7.3 is an example of a convolutional network.

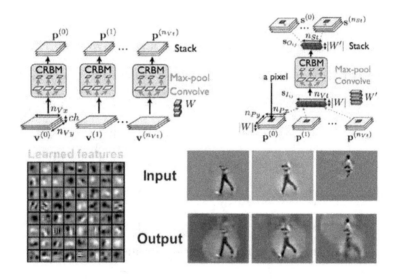

Figure 7.3. Deep Learning in Convolutional Neural Networks.

Figure 7.3 shows the deep learning method in the CNN network. CNN is the first neural network that is at the forefront of solving important commercial applications and today's commercial deep learning applications. Handwriting recognition and optical character recognition applications by Microsoft are CNN based. Although CNN has been winning computer vision contests against other machine learning years ago, Krizhevsky and his friends have demonstrated the commercial success of deep learning in 2012, when they won the first ImageNet object recognition contest.

CNN are neural networks that work successfully with deep back-trained deep networks, although back propagation networks fail. Deep Learning provides a different approach by training Deep Neural Networks (DNN) structure. In general, DNN can be trained with learning methods, with or without counseling. In advisory learning, tagged data is used for training, weights are learned by using classification or regression methods to minimize the error in estimating the target value. In consultant-free learning, training is carried out without the need for training of tagged data. In counseling learning; aggregation, feature extraction, or size reduction are often used.

7.3.2   Deep Auto-Encoders

It is a Deep Learning application that uses back-propagation learning from advisory learning algorithms used in face recognition, signal noise removal, speech recognition. Figure 7.4 is an example of Deep Auto Encoder.

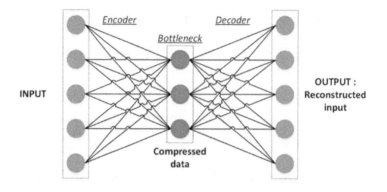

Figure 7.4.Example on deep auto encoder.

7.3.3 Restricted Boltzmann Machine (RBM)

It is a stochastic neural network modeled by Hinton et al. In 1986, by re-designing a different version of the Boltzmann Machine and using stochastic units using a particular distribution method such as Gauss distribution. These networks can be used to model probability relationships between variables.

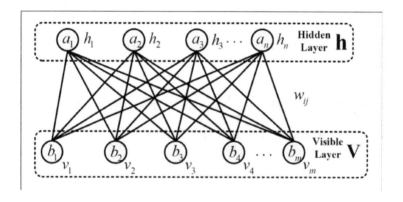

7.3.4 Deep Faith Networks (DBN)

The hidden layer of each subnet is a combination of RBMs, to which it connects to the visible layer of the next RBM. The non-directional links only have connections on the upper two layers and directed to the lower layers. Using consultant-free learning; The effective layer is a Deep Learning model with a strategy that learns with a greedy learning strategy and then adjusts based on target outcomes.

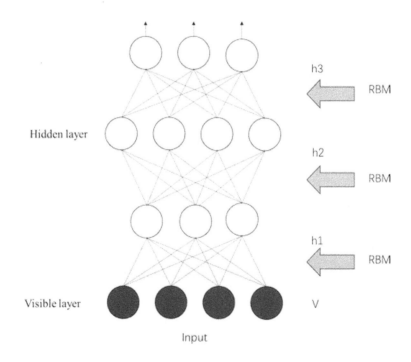

7.3.5 Deep Boltzmann Machine (DBM)

DBM proposed by Hinton and Salakhutdinov is another DNN variant based on the Boltzmann family. Its main difference from DBN is that it has administrative connections between all layers of the previous network. In this case, considering the visible units, the calculation of the posterior distribution on hidden units cannot be achieved by maximizing the probability as a result of interactions between hidden units. Therefore, in order to train DBM, a stochastic maximum probability based algorithm is used to maximize the probability lower limit. Similar to the DBN network, while training the DBM network in advance, a training strategy is implemented in the direction of the greedy layer. The main disadvantage of DBM is the complexity of time required for extraction, which is quite high compared to DBN, and makes optimization of the parameters impractical for the large training set.

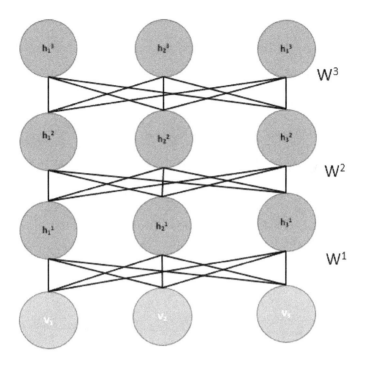

W^3

W^2

W^1

7.4 Deep Learning Applications

A study group at the University of Washington analyzed the lip movement on the face and worked in the field of image and sound synchronization. The Google Brain workgroup modeled a Deep Learning network using Pixel Recursive Super Resolution method to increase the resolution in photos at the beginning of 2017. Although the result of the study was not excellent, it was successful in predicting many characteristics of people.

The Deep Learning method can also play a helpful role in real-time multi-person exposure prediction. In their study, Zhe Cao et al. Modeled a network structure that predicts the position of the human skeletal system. The model predicted where and how the skeletal system moved by making video analysis. The Deep Learning network can be used in a study that can automatically divide the image into sections and write a short sentence that defines each section.

Andrej Karpathy and Li Fei-Fei trained a Deep Learning network in one of their works to identify dozens of interesting areas in an image and explain what happens in each area. This means that the computer has learned not only to classify the items in the photo, but also to identify them in English grammar.

In DeepWarp, Ganin and his friends trained a Deep Learning network to change one's gaze on photography.

It has the ability to assist in deep learning behavior analysis. DeepGlint is a solution used to obtain real-time information about the behavior of vehicles, people and potentially other objects using the Deep Learning method.

Nguyen and her friends have provided the Deep Learning network to synthesize new photographs from existing photographs. The network has uncovered spectacular photos of flowers, birds, faces, and more, as well as erupting volcanoes.

The Google Translate app can now automatically translate texts into a preferred language in real time. When the camera is hovered over the object to read the text, the device operates the Deep Learning network (converts it to OCR text) to read the image.

The Deep Learning network can produce new photos. For example, photos taken during the day have been converted into images that appear to be taken at night. Pix2Pix used the Deep Learning network to perform multiple tasks in Isola and similar applications.

Google Sunroof uses aerial photographs of Google Earth to create a three-dimensional model of the roof. Deep Learning Neural Networks are used to separate the roof from the surrounding trees and shadows. Then, it is estimated how much energy can be produced by installing solar panels on the roof based on the orbit of the sun and the weather patterns.

Google's DeepMind used a Deep Learning technique called Deep Reinforcement Learning to play Breakout, the Atari game. The computer is not specifically programmed to play the game in any way. Instead, control of the keyboard is given while monitoring the score. In the beginning, terrible results were obtained as the movements were mostly random; After two hours, the computer specializes in adapting to the game. The computer realized that digging a tunnel through the wall after four hours was the most effective way to beat the game.

Deep Learning groups are in a computer raising race to beat people in almost every game imaginable.

Driverless vehicles are also an example of Deep Learning applications. Driving is provided by distinguishing different types of objects, including people and road signs, with the help of the method.

Deep Learning is also used extensively in robotics these days. Two examples of Boston Dynamics robots can be given in this area: SpotMini and Atlas. Robots react to people pushing them, stand up as they fall, and can even deal with very detailed and gentle work, such as emptying the dishwasher.

Google uses WaveNet; Baidu launched Deep Speech. Both products in the subject have Deep Learning networks that automatically generate sound. Systems created today learn to imitate human voices themselves and improve over time.

An example of using a Deep Learning network to produce musical compositions can be given as an example. The work of Francesco Marchesani, who trains the computer to compose music like classical composer Chopin, can be shown in the literature. After learning the patterns and statistics specific to Chopin's music, the model creates a completely new piece.

Style transfer is a technique in which the Deep Learning network can transfer artistic styles from known artworks to new images. Egyptian hieroglyphics, Google Maps, Deep Learning style transfer technique was used to apply their styles to Mona Lisa.

Studies that turn a text into the writing style of a desired author with Deep Learning networks are available in the literature. One of the methodologies of Deep Learning, Long Short Term Memory (LSTM) performs surprisingly well in textual inputs. In an appropriate blog post by Andrej Karpathy entitled "The Irrational Effectiveness of Repetitive Neural Networks", Karpathy enabled the Deep Learning network to "read" Shakespeare, Wikipedia, mathematics documents and computer code. As a result, the model wrote articles like Shakespeare and Wikipedia.

Alex Graves from the University of Toronto has created a model with its own handwriting in a variety of styles using Deep Learning networks.

Harvard scientists used Deep Learning algorithms to perform viscoelastic calculations in earthquake prediction. However, this application increased the calculation time by 50%. The system is not considered very successful because time is very important for a problem such as earthquake.

Challenges include capture, duration, storage, research, sharing, transfer, analysis and visualization. The trend is due to large data sets due to the additional information derived from the analysis of one large set of relevant data, compared to smaller smaller groups with the same total size of data, which allows links to reveal "pivotal business trends, determine the quality of research, and link legal citations, Fight crime and define traffic conditions in real time. "

As of 2012, limits on the size of data sets appropriate for processing in a reasonable period of time were subject to the data measurement unit xb. Scientists usually encounter a number of constraints due to the huge data sets found in many fields, which include meteorology (weather science), genetics (genomics), and physical simulations. Complex and biological and environmental research, and restrictions also affect Internet search (search engine), business technology and finance. Data sets grow in size in part, due to the fact that they are increasingly collected by mobile information sensors, atmospheric sensory technologies (remote sensing), program records, cameras, microphones, and transmitters (radio frequency identification) networks and networks Wireless sensor. The global technological capacity to store information per person has nearly doubled every 40 months in the 1980s, and as of 2012, 2.5 quintillion bytes (2.5 x 1018) of data is generated daily. The challenge for large corporations is to determine who should own the big data initiatives spread across the entire organization.

It is difficult to work with big data using most relational database management systems, desktop statistics and simulation packages, instead it requires "extensive parallel software running on tens, hundreds, or even thousands of servers." What is considered "big data" varies according to the capabilities of the organization that manages the group, and the capabilities of applications that are traditionally used to process and analyze the data set in its own scope. For some organizations, facing hundreds of gigabytes of data for the first time may lead to a review of data management options. For others, it may take tens or hundreds of terabytes of data before data size becomes an important issue.

Big data usually includes data sets of sizes that go beyond the ability of commonly used programs to capture, manage and process data within an acceptable time period. As for big data volumes, it is a constantly moving target, as of 2012, its size ranges from a few dozen terabytes to many petabytes of data in only one group. With this difficulty, new platforms of "big data" tools are being developed to deal with various aspects of large amounts of data.

In a research report and a number of related lectures in 2001, Doug Lannie, analyst of META Group (now known as Gartner), defined the challenges of data growth and opportunities as a three-dimensional element, meaning increasing volume (data quantity), speed (speed of incoming and outgoing data) Diversity (diversity of data types and sources). Gartner and many companies in the industry are now continuing to use the "3Vs" model to describe big data. In 2012, Gartner updated its definition to read: "Big data is the origins of high-volume, high-speed, and / or high-diversity information assets that require new forms of processing to enhance decision-making, deep understanding, and process improvement."

TBDI definition of big data: Big data is a term that applies to big bodies of data that vary in nature whether they are organized, unorganized or semi-structured, including from internal or external sources of the organization, and are generated with a high degree of speed with a turbulent model, which does not It fully aligns with traditional and structured data warehouses and requires a robust and complex ecosystem with a high performance computing platform and analytical capabilities to capture, process, transform, detect, extract and extract value and deep insights within an acceptable time frame. "

8.1   Data Science and Big Data Analysis

Big data approach cannot be easily achieved using traditional data analysis methods. Instead, unstructured data requires specialized data modeling techniques, tools, and systems to extract insights and information as needed by organizations. Data science is a scientific approach that applies mathematical and statistical ideas and computer tools to processing big data. Data science is a specialized field that combines multiple fields such as statistics, mathematics, smart data capture technologies, data cleaning, mining and programming to prepare and align big data for smart analysis to extract visions and information.

Currently, we are all seeing unprecedented growth in information generated worldwide and on the Internet to get the big data concept. Data science is a very difficult field due to the complexities involved in integrating and applying different methods, algorithms and sophisticated programming techniques to perform smart analysis in large volumes of data. Hence, the field of data science has evolved from big data, or big data and data science are inseparable.

This concept refers to a large set of heterogeneous data from different sources and is not usually available in the standard database formats that we usually realize. Big data includes all types of data, which is structured, semi-structured, and unstructured, which can be easily found on the Internet. Big data includes:

1. Unorganized data - social networks, emails, blogs, tweets, digital photos, digital audio / video feeds, online data sources, mobile data, sensor data, web pages, etc.
2. Semi-structured - XML files, system log files, text files, etc.
3. Structured data - RDBMS (databases), OLTP, transaction data, and other structured data formats.
Therefore, all data and information regardless of type or format can be understood as big data. Big data processing usually starts with collecting data from multiple sources.

8.2   Relational Databases and Data Modeling

A data model is a method by which we can organize and store data. Just as Dewey Decimal System organizes books in a library, the data model helps us arrange data according to service, access, and use. Torvalds, Linux founder, alluded to the importance of data modeling when he wrote an article on "What Makes an Excellent Programmer": "Weak programmers care about code, and good programmers care about data structure and relationships between data." Models and appropriate storage environments provide the following benefits for big data:

1. Performance: Good data models can help us quickly query the required data and reduce the I / O rate.

2. Cost: Good data models can significantly reduce unnecessary data redundancy, reuse computing results, and reduce storage and computing costs for the big data system.

3. Efficiency: Good data models can dramatically improve user experience and increase data efficiency.

4. Quality: Good data models make data statistics more consistent and reduce the possibility of arithmetic errors.

Therefore, the big data system undoubtedly requires high-quality data modeling methods to organize and store data, which allows us to reach the optimum balance between performance, cost, efficiency and quality.

8.3 Data Warehouse and Integration

Data-Warehouse is a type of database that contains a large amount of data destined to help in making decisions within the organization. This type of database is characterized by the conformity of its internal structure with what the user needs from the indicators and axes of analysis in what is known as the star star model, and its applications: decision support systems and data mining.

Data warehouses usually contain historical data that was derived and extracted from the data in the regular databases used in applications that many input and update operations occur on, and data warehouses can also contain data from other sources such as text files and other documents. Data warehouses have the following characteristics:

1. Subject Oriented
2. Integrated Integeated
3. Nonvolatile stable
4. Time dependent

Data warehouse layers:

1- The external and operational databases layer 2- The data access layer 3- The data access layer 4- The data description layer 5- The operations management layer 6- The messaging applications layer 7- The physical data warehouse layer (physical or physical) 8- The data representation layer

Data warehouse technologies:

1- Default data warehouse-It allows the user to access data for using some tools via the data access layer

2- Central data warehouse -Contains data sources from specific job sources

3- Distributed data warehouse - Physical data distribution

Data Integration is the consolidation of data from different sources, and provides users with a unified view of this data. This process becomes of great benefit in a variety of cases, including commercial ones (for example, when two similar companies urgently need to integrate their databases) and there are scientific applications as well (such as combining the results of bioinformatics research from different repositories, for example). The importance of data synthesis is beginning to appear with increasing frequency, as the volume and need to exchange existing data has increased greatly. It became the focus of theoretical work very broad, and remains unresolved with the many open problems.

We can say that big data integration differs from traditional data integration in many dimensions: size, speed, diversity, and honesty, which are the main characteristics of big data:

1. Size (Volume): It is the original feature of Big Data. Nowadays, the number of connected devices and peoples is

higher than before, which has greatly affected the number of data sources and the amount of data worldwide.

2. Speed (Velocity): With the increase in the number of data sources, the rate of data generation has increased significantly over time, especially after the rise of social media and the use of IOT.

3. Diversity (Variety): More data sources indicate that we have more diversity in the formats that data is stored in. We have structured and unstructured data at a high level. In each type, we have a large number of formats: text, images, sounds, xml, documents, spatial data, etc.

4. Honesty (Veracity): The characteristics mentioned above, have caused us to have a different data quality, so that we can find unconfirmed or inaccurate data especially that social media and blogs allow users to publish this type of data.

8.4   Parallel Databases

A parallel database system seeks to improve performance by paralleling various processes, such as downloading data, building indexes and evaluating queries. Although data may be stored in a distributed manner, distribution is only subject to performance considerations. Parallel databases improve processing and I / O speeds using multiple CPUs and discs in parallel. Central database systems and client servers are not robust enough to handle such applications. In parallel processing, many operations are performed simultaneously, unlike sequential processing, where computational steps are performed sequentially. Parallel databases can be roughly divided into two groups, the first group of architecture is multi-processor architecture, and its alternatives are the following:

Shared memory architecture

Multiple processors share the main memory space (RAM), but each processor has its own disk (HDD). If many processes are running at one time, the speed is reduced, just like the computer when you are running many parallel tasks and the computer slows down.

Shared disk engineering

Each node has its own main memory, but all nodes share a large storage space, usually a storage area network. In practice, each node also contains multiple processors.

Architecture sharing is none

Each node has its own large storage space in addition to the main memory.

Another group of architecture is called mixed architecture, which includes:

Irregular memory architecture (NUMA), which includes access to irregular memory.

Cluster (none shared + shared disk: SAN / NAS), which consists of a group of connected computers.

In these switches or hubs, they are used to connect different computers in the cheapest and simplest way. A simple topology is used only to connect different computers. Much smarter if the switch is implemented.

8.5   Data Visualization

Big data visualization involves displaying data of almost any type in a graphical format that makes it easy to understand and interpret. But it goes far beyond typical corporate charts, pie charts and graphs to more complex representations such as thermal maps and fever charts, allowing decision makers to explore data sets to Identify unexpected correlations or patterns.

The hallmark of Big Data visualization is the scale. Today's institutions collect and store vast amounts of data that may take years for a person to read, let alone understand. But researchers have determined that the human retina can transfer data to the brain at a rate of about 10 megabits per second. Big data visualization relies on powerful computer systems to absorb and process company initial data to create a graphical representation that allows humans to absorb and understand massive amounts of data in seconds.

The volume of data created by companies around the world increases every year, and thanks to innovations such as the Internet of Things, this growth shows no sign of abating. The problem for companies is that this data is only useful if valuable insights can be extracted from and acted upon.

To do this, decision makers need to be able to access, evaluate, understand, and act upon data virtually in real time, and imagine imagining big data in a way that they can. Big data visualization is not the only way for decision makers to analyze data, but big data visualization technologies offer a fast and effective way to:

Reviewing large amounts of data - data presented in the form of graphs that enables decision makers to absorb large amounts of data and gain an understanding of what they mean very quickly - much more quickly than scrolling over spreadsheets or analyzing numerical tables.

Positional trends - Chronological data often captures trends, but it is difficult to determine hidden trends in data - especially when sources are diverse and the amount of data is large. But the use of appropriate visualization techniques for big data can make these trends easy to detect, and commercially, the trend being detected early is an opportunity to work on.

Identify unexpected connections and relationships - one of the big strengths of visualizing big data is enabling users to explore data sets - not to find answers to specific questions, but to discover unexpected visions that data can reveal. This can be done by adding or removing data sets, changing metrics, removing outliers, and changing visualization types. Identifying previously unexpected patterns and relationships in data can provide companies with a huge competitive advantage.

Show data to others - a feature that is often overlooked in visualizing big data is that it provides a very effective way to communicate any insights it shows to others. This is because it can transfer meaning very quickly and in a way that is easy to understand: specifically what is needed in both internal and external trade offers.

The human brain has evolved to accommodate and understand visual information, and excels in recognizing visual patterns. It is this ability that enables humans to discover signs of danger, as well as recognize human faces and specific human faces such as family members.

Big data visualization technologies take advantage of this by presenting data in a visual form so that it can be processed by this human-wire-solid ability almost instantly - rather than, for example, through mathematical analysis that has to be learned and applied strenuously.

The trick with visualization of big data is to choose the most effective way to visualize data to show any insights it might contain. In some circumstances, simple business tools such as pie charts or graphs may reveal the whole story, but with large, varied and diverse datasets, esoteric visualization techniques may be more appropriate. Various examples of big data visualization include:

1. Linear: Lists of items, items are arranged by one feature.

2. 2D / Level / Geospatial: mapping, point distribution maps, proportional symbol maps, contour maps.

3. 3D / Volumetric: 3D computer models, computer simulation

4. Timetable: timelines, timeline charts, connected dispersion charts, arc diagrams, pie charts.

5. Multidimensional: pie charts, graphs, clouds, bar charts, tree maps, thermal maps, spider charts.

6. Tree / Hierarchy: Schematic strips, radial tree diagrams, hyperbolic diagrams.

8.6   Social Network Analysis

Social network analysis presents social relationships in terms of network theory which consists of relationships (also called edges, links, or connections), nodes are the individual actors within networks, and the connections and relationships between actors.

Theoretical roots of social network analysis go back to the work done by early sociologists like George Semmel and Emile Durkheim, who wrote about the importance of studying the patterns of relationships that link social actors. Sociologists have used the concept of "social networks" since the beginnings of the twentieth century to denote complex groups of relationships between members belonging to social systems at all levels, from personal relationships to international ones. Both Jacob L. Moreno and Helen Hall Jennings basic analytical methods in the 1930s. John Arundel began in 1954 to use the term systematically to denote link patterns that include concepts traditionally used by the public, and those used by sociologists: limited social groups (such as tribes and families) and social groups (such as gender and ethnicity).

Researchers have expanded - such as Ronald Burt, Kathleen Carly, Mark Granovetter, David Crackhardt, Edward Laumann, Anatole Report, Barry Wolman and Douglas R. White and Harrison White - The use of structured social network analysis applied even in literary studies by Anaheim, Gerhards, Romo, Water de Nuclear, and Birgit Senegal. Social network analysis actually found applications in various academic disciplines as well as practical applications such as counter-terrorism and money laundering.

Practical applications

Social network analysis is widely used in a wide range of applications and disciplines. Common network analysis applications include aggregation, data mining, network propagation modeling, network modeling, sampling, user characteristics, behavior analysis, community resource support, site-based interaction analysis, social sharing, filtering, recommendation system development, link prediction, and entity resolution. Companies in the private sector use social network analysis to support activities such as scientists 'interactions, analyzes, information system development and marketing analysis, and business intelligence needs. Some uses of the public sector include developing strategies for engaging leaders, analyzing individual and group participation, using media, and solving social problems.

Security applications

Social network analysis is also used in intelligence, counter-espionage and law enforcement activities. This technology allows analysts to designate secret organizations such as a spy gang, organized crime family, or street gang. The National Security Agency uses its own secret digital spy software to generate the data necessary to conduct this type of analysis on terrorist cells and other networks that are considered to be relevant to national security. The NSA is looking for three deep nodes during this network analysis, after the initial social network planning is completed, and the analysis is done to determine the network's structure and to identify leaders within it, for example. This measure permits military assets or law enforcement to launch head-attacks or killings of targets with high-ranking positions to disrupt the network's operation. The National Security Agency began conducting social network analysis on call detail records, also known as metadata, shortly after the September 11 attacks.

Textual analysis applications

Large text companies can be converted to networks and then analyzed using the social network analysis method. The nodes in these networks are social actors and the links are actions. These networks can be automated extracting using analyzers. The resulting networks that can contain thousands of nodes are then analyzed using tools from network theory, to identify the main actors, major societies or parties, and general characteristics such as durability or the structural stability of the public or central network of a particular node. This automates the approach presented by quantitative narrative analysis, as it defines triads (being, verb and actor) with pairs of actors associated with an action or pairs consisting of (object and actor).

data mining is a computerized and manual search for knowledge of data without prior assumptions about what that knowledge might be. Data mining is also defined as the process of analyzing a quantity of data (usually a large amount), to find a logical relationship that summarizes the data in a new way that is understandable and useful to the owner of the data. "Models" are called relationships and summarized data obtained from data mining. Data mining usually deals with data that has been obtained for a purpose other than the purpose of data mining (for example, a database of transactions in a bank), which means that the method of data mining does not affect the way the data itself is collected. This is one of the areas in which data mining differs from statistics, and for this the data mining process is referred to as a secondary statistical process. The definition also indicates that the amount of data is usually large, but if the amount of data is small, it is preferable to use regular statistical methods in analyzing it.

When dealing with a large volume of data, new issues arise such as how to identify the distinct points in the data, how to analyze the data in a reasonable period of time and how to decide whether any apparent relationship reflects a fact in the nature of the data. Usually data is excavated that is part of the entire data, where the purpose is usually to generalize the results to all data (for example, analyzing the current data of consumers of a product in order to anticipate future consumer demands). One of the goals of data mining is also to reduce or compress large amounts of data to express simple data without generalization.

9.1   Data Mining Techniques

Data mining includes the use of revised data analysis tools to find previously unknown patterns and valid relationships in massive data sets. These tools can include statistical models, machine learning techniques and mathematical algorithms, such as neural networks or decision trees. Thus, data mining includes analysis and forecasting.

Depending on the different methods and techniques from the intersection of machine learning, database management, and statistics, data mining professionals have dedlcated their functions to a better understanding of how to process and extract an enormous amount of data, but what methods do they use to achieve this?

In recent data mining projects, several key data mining and development techniques have been developed and developed, including correlation, classification, aggregation, prediction, chain patterns, and regression.

1. Classification:

This technology is used to obtain important and relevant information about data and metadata. This data mining technology helps group data into different categories.

Data extraction techniques can be classified according to different criteria, as follows:

Classification of data extraction frameworks by type of mined data sources:

This classification is based on the type of data being handled. For example, multimedia, spatial data, text data, time series data, global network, etc.

Classifying data mining frameworks according to the relevant database:

This classification is based on the respective data model. For example. Object-oriented database, transactional database, relational database, etc.

Classification of data mining frameworks by type of knowledge discovered:

This classification depends on the types of knowledge discovered or data mining functions. For example, discrimination, classification, grouping, descriptions, etc. Some frameworks tend to be comprehensive frameworks that offer some data mining functions together.

Classify data extraction frameworks according to the data mining techniques used:

This classification is according to the data analysis methodology used, such as neural networks, machine learning, genetic algorithms, visualization, statistics, data warehouse or database router, etc.

Classification can also take into account the level of user interaction involved in a data mining procedure, such as query-dependent systems, standalone systems, or interactive mining systems.

2. Clustering:

Clustering is the division of information into groups of connected objects. Describing data by a few groups mainly loses some confined details, but accomplishes improvement. It model data by its collections. Data modeling places aggregation from a historical point of view rooted in statistics, mathematics and numerical analysis.

From the perspective of machine learning, groups are associated with hidden patterns, the search for groups is learning without supervision, and the next frame represents the concept of data. From a business point of view, agglomeration plays an exceptional job in data mining applications. For example, scientific data mining, text mining, information retrieval, spatial database applications, customer relationship management, web analysis, computational biology, medical diagnostics, and much more.

In other words, we can say that clustering analysis is a data mining technique for identifying similar data. This technique helps to identify differences and similarities between the data. Aggregation is very similar to categorization, but it involves grouping large pieces of data together based on similarities between them.

3. Regression:

Regression analysis is the process of extracting data used to define and analyze the relationship between variables due to the presence of the other factor. It is used to determine the probability of the specified variable. Regression is primarily a form of planning and modeling. For example, we may use it to drop certain costs, depending on other factors such as availability, consumer demand, and competition. Primarily it gives the exact relationship between two or more variables in a given data set.

4. Assembly rules:

This data mining technology helps discover the connection between two or more elements. Finds a hidden pattern in the data set.

Pairing rules are if-then statements that support showing the possibility of interaction between data elements within large data sets in different types of databases. Link base mining contains many applications and is commonly used to help sales links in medical data or data sets.

The way the algorithm works is that you have different data, for example, a list of grocery items that you have been purchasing for the past six months. Calculates the percentage of items purchased together.

5. External examination:

This type of data mining technology relates to monitoring data elements in the data set, which do not match the expected pattern or expected behavior. This technology can be used in various fields such as intrusion, detection, fraud detection, etc. Also known as external analysis or external mining. The exterior is a data point that is very different from the rest of the data set. The vast majority of data sets in the real world have an out. Outside disclosure plays an important role in the field of data mining. External detection is valuable in many areas such as determining network outages, detecting credit or debit card fraud, detecting remote in wireless sensor network data, etc.

6. Sequential patterns:

Sequential pattern is a specialized data extraction technique for evaluating chain data to discover chain patterns. It consists of finding interesting sequences in a series of sequences, in which the sequence share can be measured in terms of different criteria such as length, frequency of occurrence, etc.

In other words, this data mining technology helps discover or recognize similar patterns in transaction data over a period of time.

7. Prediction:

The prediction used a host of other data mining techniques such as trends, groups, classification, etc. It analyzes past events or states in the correct sequence to predict a future event.

1. Anomaly detection

Anomalous detection can be used to determine when something is significantly different from a normal pattern.

2. Union learning

Associated learning or market basket analysis is used to analyze things that tend to happen together either in pairs or in larger groups.

3. Block detection

Identifying distinct groups or subcategories within data is known as cluster detection. Machine learning algorithms discover different subsets significantly in a data set.

4. Classification

Unlike mass detection, the classification deals with things that already have stickers. This is referred to as training data - when there is information present that can be trained on an algorithm or easily categorized.

5. Regression

The regression method is used to make relationship-based predictions within a data set. As mentioned above, Facebook's future interaction can be expected based on everything in the user's log - likes, photo tags, comments, interactions with other users, friend requests, and all other activities on the site.

9.3   Data Mining Process

1. Data cleaning: Inconsistent and erroneous data in the database is called noise. To clear the noise in the data; records containing missing values can be discarded, a fixed value can be assigned instead of missing values, this value can be written instead of missing data by calculating the average of other data, and can be used instead of missing data by making an appropriate estimate (decision tree, regression).

2. Data integration: It is the process of converting different types of data into one type so that the data obtained from different databases or data sources can be evaluated together. The most common example of this is seen in gender. It is a data that can be kept in many types and it can be kept as 0/1 in one database, while it can be kept as E / K or Male / Female in the other database. Success in the discovery of information also depends on the compatibility of the data.

3. Data reduction: If data mining applications are believed to be unchanged from analysis, the number of data or the number of variables can be reduced. Data reduction methods; data compression, sampling, generalization, concatenation or data cube, size reduction.

4. Data Conversion: It is the process of transforming the shape of the data by preserving its content according to the model to be used. The conversion should be done in accordance with the model to be used. Because the model and algorithm to be used in the display of the data play an important role. If the average and variances of the variables are significantly different from each other, the variables with large average and variance will have more pressure on the others and significantly reduce their roles. Therefore, normalization should be done on the data.

5. Apply the data mining algorithm: After the data is ready, data mining algorithms are applied.

6. Presentation and evaluation of the results: After the algorithms are applied, the results are arranged and presented to the relevant places. For example, if the hierarchical clustering method is applied, the results are presented with a dendrogram chart.

9.4 Data Mining Methods

1. Classification: Classification is the area where data mining is used the most. Classification rules are created by using some of the existing database as education. With the help of these rules, how to decide when a new situation arises is determined. The most frequently used technical decision trees in the classification group of data mining. Logistic regression, discriminant analysis, neural networks and fuzzy sets are also used. Classification can be used both as a basis for data mining and as a tool for data preparation, as people always classify, categorize and rate data.

2. Clustering: It is the process of grouping the data by considering the similarities among them and most of the clustering methods use the distances between the data. Hierarchical Clustering methods are the closest neighbor algorithm and the farthest neighbor algorithm. Many clustering methods are used in practice. These methods are used to subdivide a cluster using the similarities or differences between the variables. Although the technique used depends on the number of clusters, it is much more useful to use both techniques together. Thus, it is possible to compare both the results and which of the two techniques give more suitable results. The purpose of cluster analysis is to classify ungrouped data according to their similarities and to assist the researcher in obtaining summative information. Although the assumption is that the data is normally distributed to apply cluster analysis, this assumption remains in theory and is ignored in applications. It is only satisfied with the suitability of distance values for normal distribution. If this assumption is met, a different assumption is not required for the Covariance matrix in cluster analysis.

3. Association Rules: These are data mining methods that try to reveal which events can occur simultaneously by examining the relationships of records in the database. It is especially applied in marketing (market basket analysis). These methods reveal the rules of coexistence with certain possibilities. The most common application of partnership analysis is done to determine the buying tendencies of the customers in retail sales. The applications that reveal the tendency of the customers by considering all the products they buy at once are called "Market Basket Analysis". For example; To say that 60% of customers who buy perfumes

240

from a store purchase perfumes in the same shop can be an example of these events that take place together.

9.5 Text Mining

Text mining, sometimes referred to alternately as text data mining, which roughly means text analysis, indicates the process of extracting high-quality information from text. The extraction of high-quality information is through division of patterns and trends through means such as statistical learning of patterns. Prospecting usually requires the structuring of the entered text (usually an analysis, along with the addition of some derivative language features and the removal of others, and then inclusion in a database), extracting patterns in structured data, and finally evaluating and interpreting the outcome. 'High Quality' in the field of textual mining usually indicates a mixture of relevance, modernity, and interest. Typical tasks for prospecting in texts include categorizing texts, compiling text, extracting concepts, producing granular classifications, sentiment analysis, document summarization, and modeling relationships between entities (i.e. learning relationships between named entities).

For example, text mining may relate to indexing texts in relation to the words they contain and this is the simplest text mining application. Then we can ask the index through keywords to know the similarities between it and the list of texts. The indexing algorithm can be configured as follows:

Index the text for the words it contains.

Reverse indexing (indexing words relative to texts).

When analyzing the query question for the index consisting of semantic words, we calculate the similarity between it and the reverse indexing of texts.

This gives us the order of the texts according to their similarity with the keywords raised.

Many textual mining applications start from indexing for search engines to extracting knowledge from unstructured texts. There are some techniques such as converting words into trunks that enable us to develop indexing while losing some meaning in return.

9.6   Web Mining

The World Wide Web, or simply the web, is one of the world's largest sources of information. We can say, perhaps, that any topic we think of is likely to be found on a page on the web. Information on the Internet comes in various forms and types such as text documents, photos and videos.

However, extracting information is useful, without the help of some web tools, not an easy process. This is where web mining comes in, which provides tools that help us extract useful knowledge from web data. In this research article, I will present an overview of web mining with a focus on textual data, a brief description of the web properties that make mining of great importance, what constitutes data mining, and some future directions for this field.

In the computer world, data is an interesting field. It is constantly increasing and expanding greatly, and it is important for us to find useful information from this big data. The comprehensive process of analyzing data sets, to find understandable and useful information for data owners, is called data mining. In the past few years, most enterprise-owned data has been stored in structured data stores such as relational databases. This data is easily accessible for mining purposes using many data mining techniques. However, the nature of the data has changed dramatically since the advent of the Internet, which has advantages and characteristics that make it different from structured data. These characteristics can be summarized as follows:

> 1. The huge volume of data on the web is still growing exponentially.

2. The web contains data of various types and shapes. This includes structured data like a table, semi-structured data like XML documents, non-structured data like text in webpages, and multimedia data like pictures and movies.

3. The heterogeneity of information on the Internet. Authors from around the world participate in building web content. as a result. You may find pages with similar or identical content.

4. Web data has hyperlinks, which means that web pages link together so that anyone can navigate through pages within the site itself or across different sites. These links can tell us how information is organized between pages within the site, and how strong or weak the relationship between pages is across different sites.

5. Noise information on the web. The reasons for this are two issues. First, a typical webpage usually contains many information such as the main body of the page, links, ads, and many more. Thus, the page has no specific structure. Second, there is no

qualitative control over the information, meaning that anyone can upload content to the web regardless of quality or quality.

6. A large portion of the content on the Internet is dynamic, which means that the information is updated frequently and continuously. For example, the weather information is constantly updated.

7. The web contains e-commerce sites that enable people to make many purchases, transfer money, and many more. This type of site needs to provide customers with computerized services such as a recommendation system.

8. The web is not just data and information. Nowadays, the web is a virtual community, where people, organizations, and even computerized systems can communicate and interact with one another. All these characteristics make the process of extracting data on the network more challenging, while giving us opportunities to discover useful and valuable knowledge from the web. With a wide range of data types, traditional data mining techniques have become insufficient. This led to the

crystallization of a need to develop new technologies and algorithms aimed at data mining on the Internet.

9.6.1   Web Structure Mining

By web architecture, we mean using the web hyperlink architecture as a source of information in the prospecting process. Hyperlinks represent one of the special features of the network as well as the basis of the web. All web pages are linked to each other by links so that the user can move from one page to another through it. Web Structure Mining aims to extract useful, abstract knowledge of a hyperlink structure on a network for various purposes. Some of the technologies used in exploring the web architecture are inspired by the analysis of social networks through which we can find certain types of pages such as axes, powers, and societies based on incoming and outgoing links. In the following paragraphs, I will briefly discuss some of the tasks of exploring the web architecture with their techniques.

1. Web Search Results Optimization

Extracting knowledge from the hyperlink structure is very important for search engines so that relevant web pages can be discovered. In primitive online search engines, information retrieval methods alone were insufficient to rank the results returned by search engines on the web. With hyperlinks present, the researchers found that the results retrieved could be significantly improved.

2. Discover societies

A network architecture can also be used to discover a group of content contributors, or so-called community users, who share common interests; Each community can be seen as a set of related web pages. There are three main reasons why societies can discover:

1. Communities often have the most valuable, relevant, and up-to-date information for the users involved in that information.

2. Societies make the Internet more social, and people who are interested in the intellectual development of the web can study these societies.

3. Societies can serve targeted advertisements on a very precise level. Such societies can be extracted using the aforementioned HITS algorithm. In short, the Hits algorithm can find what are called the main subjective vectors, which represent the most dense regions containing powers and hubs.

By web content mining, we use the contents of webpages to extract useful information. Sorting and grouping webpages according to their topics are examples of tasks that fall within web content mining. These tasks are similar to those used to extract traditional data. However, there are tasks on the internet that are not considered traditional extraction tasks. Examples include extracting customer opinions from customer reviews and social network posts, extracting product specifications as well as analyzing sentiments and many more. In the following paragraphs, I will briefly discuss the main tasks used in exploring web content.

1. Structured data extraction: collector generation

One of the obvious problems we face when extracting information is extracting information items from web pages. Extracting information from natural language text is widely studied by natural language processing societies (NLP). The challenge from a web mining perspective is to extract structured data from web pages.

The program that aims to extract this data is called aggregator. Structured data is represented on the Internet by entering data retrieved from the primary structured data source, which usually appears on web pages through tables and templates. Increasingly, many organizations may publish their data on their websites, and it has become important to extract this data for many purposes such as: customizable information gathering on the web, product comparison, meta-search and many others. There are many methods used to build this complex. Liu outlines three approaches:

1. Manual Approach: This approach relies entirely on human programmers by monitoring a webpage and source code. Then the programmer extracts the rules and then develops a program based on these rules to extract the targeted information. This approach is obviously not able to accommodate other different pages.

2. Collector extrapolation: This approach relies on learning methods within previously known data, where rules are learned from pre-described pages or data records. These rules are then applied to similar formats for extracting data items. An example of a system based on this approach is the Stalker system.

3. Automatic extraction: This approach overcomes pre-labeling efforts manually. It relies on uncensored learning methods, in which the databases of data elements are extracted. An example of this technology is IEPAD.

2. Information integrity

In the previous section, we briefly discussed how to extract data on the Internet and store it in a structured data source. However, collecting data from a large number of websites on the Internet adds another dimension of complexity: data integrity. Through integration, we basically mean two things:

1. Matching columns in different tables that contain the same type of data.

2. Match values that are semantic identical, but that are represented differently in different places.

In general, data integrity has been extensively studied in the context of relational databases and data warehouse; A lot of web-related information integrity research has dealt with the integration of web query interfaces. However, many of the ideas that have already been developed can be applied to data extracted from the web as well.

The main problem with information integrity is known as schema matching. It aims to produce one general scheme from two or more different plans. Before the chart matching process, it usually requires pre-processing steps to be taken including: subdivision, expansion, standardization of words, and pausing words removal.

Basically, there are different types of matching as suggested by Ram and Bernstein:

1. Matching scheme only: Only chart information such as names and data types are approved.

2. Matching field and data only: The data is approved with the field information for each column.

3. Matching chart, field, and data: Evidence is approved with field information for each column in addition to chart information.

There are several methods for all of the above. The second type, which is domain and data only, is the most common case on the web because the schema is often hidden. The third type is usually a combination of the first two techniques. A more detailed discussion of these methods can be found at.

3. Seek opinions and analyze feelings

As part of the web contains structured data, it also contains a massive amount of unstructured data. This data is usually unstructured text. One of the important web content mining tasks that handle this data is opinion mining, which strips positive or negative feelings. Social media is growing rapidly on the internet including vacancies, reviews, blogs, forums, and social networking sites like Facebook and Twitter. This content is of great importance to many individuals and institutions and helps them make decisions. Individuals can find many references to some products on the Internet. Institutions are usually interested in knowing their clients 'opinions of information publicly available on the Internet.

9.6.3   Web Use Mining

Internet usage mining refers to the process of discovering patterns of use of data on the web. The raw data used in this process is represented by usage logs, which record user-website interactions. This includes data such as user clicks, arrival date and time, IP addresses, etc. Usage logs are usually present on servers as are server logs and web application logs. Similar to the data extraction process, the internet mining process is often divided into 3 phases: pre-processing, pattern detection, and pattern analysis.

252

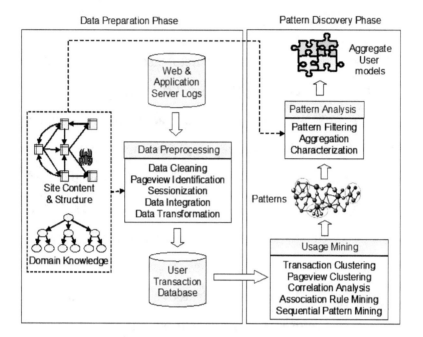

In the first, pre-processing, usage data is converted to abstractions, which represent interactions for a user within the website. Other types of data may be shared at this stage including real data on site pages, data describing the structure of web pages, and data that represents demographic information about users.

In the pattern detection stage, a wide range of methods and techniques are applied from various fields such as statistics, data mining, databases, and machine learning to reveal hidden patterns that carry user behaviors.

Examples of techniques and methods used in this type of mining are as follows:

1. Statistical analysis: Using the different statistical methods, we can find many variables that interest us such as: page browsing, pages that are accessed most of the time, the display time of pages, and the lengths of the navigation paths.

2. Link creation rules: Generating such rules can be used to link pages or items that have been accessed or purchased frequently by users. Thus, web designers are helped to efficiently organize the content of their websites.

3. Blocking: By using blocking technologies, we can discover two groups: user groups and page groups. User groups who have the same browsing patterns can be very helpful for marketing teams, for example, to provide them with personalized content.

4. Sequencing patterns: By exploring sequencing patterns, we can learn about the frequent navigation paths of users. An example of such mining would be something like "On the H Carriers website, only 10% of users visited the homepage, then the job page, and finally the demo page."

11 REFERENCES

Assis. Lect. Mohammed Ridha Faisal (2020) Step by step web design with visual studio 2019.

Dr.Öğr.Üyesi Atınç Yılmaz, Öğr.Gör. Umut Kaya (2019) Derin öğrenme

Yrd. Doç . Dr. İbrahim Küçükkoç (2018) Optimizasyon Teknikleri.

Miguel ´A. (2019) Optimization.

Doç.Dr. Metin Türkay, OPTİMİZASYON MODELLERİ VE ÇÖZÜM METODLARI

M.A. Yükselen, EĞRİ UYDURMA VE İNTERPOLASYON

İbrahim Çayıroğlu, Görüntü İşleme Ders Notları

www.elektrik.gen.tr

ar.wikipedia.org

ninova.itu.edu.tr

www.javatpoint.com

ocw.mit.edu

www.tutorialspoint.com

plato.stanford.edu

Your right way to learn web design

Source Code
Free Download

Step by step
web design with
visual studio 2019

Mohammed Ridha Faisal

Abdullah Ridha Faisal

HTML5	Web Design
CSS3	Web Design Tools
JavaScript	WebSite Construction
jQuery	Visual Studio 2019 Shortcuts

Amazon

Web design with visual studio

Amazon

Step by Step
Web Design with
Visual Studio 2017

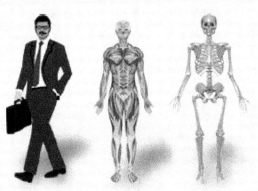

Mohammed Ridha Faisal

HTML5	Web Design
CSS3	Web Design Tools
JavaScript	Website Construction
jQuery	Visual Studio 2017 shortcuts

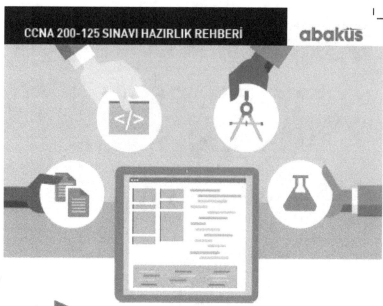

Visual Studio
ile Adım Adım
Web Tasarımı

Mohammed Ridha FAISAL

- HTML5
- CSS3
- JavaScript

- jQuery
- WEB TASARIMI
- WEB TASARIM ARAÇLARI

261

www.ingramcontent.com/pod-product-compliance
Lightning Source LLC
LaVergne TN
LVHW051732050326
832903LV00023B/891